Staffordshire Library and Information Service
Please return or renew or by the last date shown

If not required by other readers, this item may be renewed
in person, by post or telephone, online or by email.
To renew, either the book or ticket are required

24 Hour Renewal Line
0845 33 00 740

Staffordshire
County Council

D1549670

ISAAC ROSENBERG was born in Bristol on 25 November 1890, to Jewish immigrant parents from Lithuania. His family moved to the East End of London in 1897, and after a rudimentary education Rosenberg at 14 was apprenticed to an engraver. Wealthy patrons enabled him to study at the Slade School of Art (1911–14) and for nine months in 1914–15 he lived in South Africa. The only poems to be collected in his lifetime were self-published in pamphlet form – *Night and Day* (1912), *Youth* (1915) and *Moses* (1916). Enlisting in the Army in October 1915 he served on the Western Front until his death on night patrol on 1 April 1918.

It is astonishing that as a private soldier in the trenches he managed to write at all. Yet he sent home to regular correspondents, including established literary figures such as Edward Marsh, Laurence Binyon and Lascelles Abercrombie, lively letters and poems (scribbled in pencil on scraps of paper) that were among the greatest of the war. He did see his poems published in *Poetry* (*Chicago*) and Marsh's *Georgian Poetry 1916–17*. Another mentor poet, Gordon Bottomley, edited the first *Selected Poems* in 1922 and co-edited *The Collected Works of Isaac Rosenberg*, with a foreword by Siegfried Sassoon (Chatto & Windus, 1937).

JEAN LIDDIARD read English at Cambridge and subsequently worked at the Imperial War Museum, the National Portrait Gallery and the National Gallery. Her biography *The Half Used Life: Isaac Rosenberg Poet and Painter 1890–1918* was published in 1975 and she organised two exhibitions on Rosenberg, for the National Book League in 1975 (also writing the catalogue) and at the Imperial War Museum in 1990, to mark the poet's centenary. She also co-authored *Working for Victory? Images of Women in the First World War* (1987). Her edition of Rosenberg's *Selected Poems and Letters* was published by Enitharmon Press in 2003.

Self Portrait in a Felt Hat (1914–15, private collection).

Isaac Rosenberg

Poetry Out of My Head and Heart

Unpublished letters & poem versions

Edited and introduced by
Jean Liddiard

ENITHARMON PRESS
in association with

ejps

THE EUROPEAN JEWISH PUBLICATIONS SOCIETY

First published in 2007
by Enitharmon Press
26B Caversham Road
London NW5 2DU

in association with
The European Jewish Publications Society
PO Box 19948, London N3 3ZJ

*The European Jewish Publications Society is a registered charity which
gives grants to assist in the publication and distribution of books relevant
to Jewish literature, history, religion, philosophy, politics and culture.*

Distributed in the UK by
Central Books
99 Wallis Road
London E9 5LN

Distributed in the USA and Canada
by Dufour Editions Inc.
PO Box 7, Chester Springs
PA 19425, USA

ISBN: 978-1-904634-38-6

Enitharmon Press gratefully acknowledges the financial support
of Arts Council England, London.

British Library Cataloguing-in-Publication Data.
A catalogue record for this book is available
from the British Library.

Designed and typeset in Albertina by Libanus Press
and printed in England by
Cromwell Press Ltd

To the memory of Isaac Horvitch and Annie Wynick, whose unstinting support of Isaac Rosenberg's reputation has preserved his work for the enjoyment of future generations

Acknowledgements

The British Library: The Isaac Rosenberg Collection, Department of Western Manuscripts.

Bernard Wynick, Literary Executor of the Isaac Rosenberg estate.

The generosity and support of the Rosenberg family and their descendants have ensured the growth of Rosenberg's reputation and the survival of his work, as well as a permanent place for it to be available to the public at the British Library, the British Museum and the Imperial War Museum, with two self-portraits at Tate Britain and the National Portrait Gallery.

My particular gratitude is due to Rosenberg's two nephews and literary executors, firstly the late Isaac Horvitch and currently Bernard Wynick, Annie Wynick's son. I would also like especially to thank Jamie Anderson, Sally Brown and Christopher Fletcher and their colleagues from the British Library, Frances Carey of the British Museum and Roderick Suddaby of the Imperial War Museum. I also appreciate the support of Dr Vivien Noakes and her definitive scholarly work on Rosenberg.

Finally I must acknowledge the deep friendship of Mitzi Horvitch and her late husband Isaac over many years, the sympathetic suggestions of Dr Erika Langmuir, the patient support of my publisher Stephen Stuart-Smith, and the unfailing help and interest of my husband Michael Collinson.

JEAN LIDDIARD

Contents

List of main publications cited with abbreviations

PPIR. *Poems and Plays of Isaac Rosenberg*, edited by Vivien Noakes (Oxford: Oxford University Press, 2004)

SPL. Isaac Rosenberg, *Selected Poems and Letters*, edited and introduced by Jean Liddiard (London: Enitharmon Press, 2003)

CW79. *Collected Works of Isaac Rosenberg: Poetry, Prose, Letters, Paintings and Drawings*, edited with an introduction by Ian Parsons; foreword by Siegfried Sassoon (London: Chatto & Windus, 1979)

CW37. *Collected Works of Isaac Rosenberg: Poetry, Prose, Letters, and Some Drawings*, edited by Gordon Bottomley and Denys Harding; foreword by Siegfried Sassoon (London: Chatto & Windus, 1937)

PR22. *Poems by Isaac Rosenberg*, edited by Gordon Bottomley; memoir by Laurence Binyon (London: William Heinemann, 1922)

Foreword

My uncle Isaac Rosenberg was born in Bristol on 25 November 1890, and was killed while on night patrol with the King's Own Royal Lancasters in France on 1 April 1918. He was just twenty-seven and five months old. My mother Minnie, his elder sister, grieved for him for the rest of her life.

Isaac's father Barnett fled from Lithuania, then part of Russia, to avoid persecution and being forced into the army, where Jews had a hard time. He arrived in Bristol in the late 1880s. A few years later Minnie, then about three years old, came to Bristol with her mother to join her father. After seven years or so the family, then of five children, moved to London's East End, where there was a large Jewish immigrant community, and where Barnett thought it would be easier to get work. But he was untrained and had no business aptitude. He failed to find work, and ended up pulling a barrow around London. It fell to my grandmother to eke out a living for the family. As a result the family was very, very poor.

Isaac showed artistic promise when at school and then started to write poetry. It is doubtful whether he learned anything about poetry or poets at school. The ability to draw and write poetry came naturally to him. Isaac would scour the second-hand bookstalls then lining the Farringdon Road in London's East End for books about poetry and poets. My mother gave this description of him in a brief unpublished memoir: 'My brother was a sad and discontented child. He would never talk about school to his family, so after some time I went to see his teacher. The teacher said . . . he [Isaac] seemed to take little interest in anything but drawing. At playtime when all the other children were in [the playground], he remained in the classroom drawing. He didn't make friends with any of the other children and seemed too serious for his age.'

My parents named me Isaac in his memory when I was born, about two-and a-half years after he was killed. He has always been a great influence on me. Some of his paintings and drawings always hung on the walls of our home in South Africa, and my parents gave me and my sisters copies of the booklets of poetry, including a copy of his self-published play *Moses*, as well as the 1922 edition of his poetry,* and the first *Collected Works.*† I treasure them.

Isaac was a loner and shy, but in the early 1900s he met a few young East End boys who were also culturally minded. They discussed art and literature, especially poetry, and went to the theatres, walking all the way from the East End to the West End of London and back. Joseph Leftwich, later a poet and man of letters, was one of this group, and became a close friend of Isaac's. Leftwich kept a diary (in minute handwriting) in the early 1900s, and wrote about Isaac, '[He is] . . . running away to the libraries whenever he can, to read poetry and the lives of the poets, their letters, their essays on how to write poetry, their theories of what poetry should be and do . . . poetry is his obsession – not literature but essentially, distinctively poetry.'‡

Isaac's drawing and painting was also self-taught. Only later did he attend night classes at Birkbeck College. On one occasion Leftwich went to fetch Isaac at his home. He was quite shocked by what he saw, and said in his diary, 'Rosenberg was drawing in the kitchen at a corner of a rickety table, which was littered with crockery, there was hardly room to move' (Leftwich, op. cit.). He remarked that Rosenberg's parents seemed very poor. Isaac painted several self-portraits with a mirror propped up on this rickety table. It is said that he liked to paint himself, but I doubt that. It was simply that he had no other sitters. In 1904 the family prevailed upon him to leave school, and take a job. He was apprenticed to Carl Hentschel, a firm of engravers. He hated it.

The family could see that he was determined to be an artist, though

---

* *Poems by Isaac Rosenberg*, edited by Gordon Bottomley with a memoir by Laurence Binyon (London: William Heinemann, 1922) [PR22].
† *Collected Works of Isaac Rosenberg: Poetry, Prose, Letters, and Some Drawings*, edited by Gordon Bottomley and Denys Harding; foreword by Siegfried Sassoon (London: Chatto & Windus, 1937) [CW37].
‡ Joseph Leftwich, unpublished diary, 12 February 1911.

they badly needed him to earn money to help the family. My grandmother and my mother took him to meet the established artist John H. Amschewitz, who lived nearby. Amschewitz befriended Isaac, and painted a portrait of him. It was at Amschewitz's studio that he met Winifreda Seaton, a middle-aged schoolteacher, who became his confidante. He wrote to her during his apprentice years, 'it is horrible to think that all these hours, when my days are full of vigour, and my hands and soul craving for self expression, I am bound, chained to this fiendish mangling machine, without hope and almost desire of deliverance, and the days of youth go by.'* He could not stand it so he left in 1911, even though he had no work and no money.

My mother Minnie often spent evenings at the Whitechapel Library with her friends. One evening she took Isaac with her and introduced him to the librarian Morley Dainow. Dainow encouraged him, criticized his poetry, took him to the National Gallery and other art galleries, and suggested that he copy Old Masters. It was while he was painting in the National Gallery that two wealthy Jewish ladies, who happened to be in the gallery, came over to see what he was painting, and were impressed. They got talking to him, and eventually towards the end of 1911 decided to sponsor him to attend the Slade School of Art, probably the leading London art school at that time.

Isaac did well at the Slade. He said that the régime was strict, but he had a prickly relationship with his sponsors over how hard he was working. There is a photograph of the Slade Picnic 1912, and a number of the students in it became famous: David Bomberg and Mark Gertler (fellow East Enders whom Isaac already knew quite well), Dorothy Brett, Dora Carrington, C. R. W. Nevinson, and Stanley Spencer whom Isaac called 'Cookham'.

But Isaac is kneeling at one side, slightly separated from the others – possibly because of his shyness. He wrote to a fellow Slade student, Ruth Lowy, 'I have a dread of meeting people who know I write, as they expect me to talk and I am a horrible bad talker. I am in absolute

* *Collected Works of Isaac Rosenberg: Poetry, Prose, Letters, Paintings and Drawings*, edited with an introduction by Ian Parsons; foreword by Siegfried Sassoon (London: Chatto & Windus, 1979), p. 180 [CW79].

agonies in company and it needs a sympathetic listener like yourself to put me at ease' (CW79, p. 186). When I was quite young Amschewitz told me of an occasion which illustrates Isaac's personality. Isaac had come to see him in a highly excited state and said, 'Mr Amschewitz, Mr Amschewitz, I would like to read you a poem I have just written.' With that he searched his pockets furiously but could not find it and said, 'Great Snakes! I must have forgotten to write it down.'

Sometime in 1912, Isaac wrote to Laurence Binyon, who was a poet and curator in the Department of Prints and Drawings at the British Museum. He sent Binyon some of his poems, asking for criticism. Binyon invited him to the British Museum, and in his introductory memoir recalled the meeting:

> Small in stature, dark, bright-eyed, thoroughly Jewish in type, he seemed a boy with an unusual mixture of self-reliance and modesty. Indeed, no one could have had a more independent nature. Obviously sensitive, he was not touchy or aggressive. Possessed of vivid enthusiasms, he was shy in speech. One found in talk how strangely fresh a mind he brought to what he saw and read. There was an odd kind of charm in his manner which came from his earnest, transparent sincerity. [PR22, pp. 3–5]

Binyon also wrote that Isaac brought him 'a sort of autobiography . . . the story of a youth, mentally ambitious, introspective, dissatisfied with his surroundings, consumed by secret desires for liberation and self-expression' (op. cit.). Unfortunately, this document is lost, and Isaac may have destroyed it. Isaac now became especially interested in writing poetry, but never discussed his painting or poetry with his family.

He had written to Miss Seaton in 1911, 'I've discovered I'm a very bad talker: I find it difficult to make myself intelligible at times; I can't remember the exact word I want, and I think I leave the impression of being a rambling idiot' (CW79, p. 182). The difficulty he had in getting his work published may have been due to this shyness, or to his lowly origins. The poet Ezra Pound refers to these when he recommended

Isaac's work to Harriet Monroe, editor of the American magazine *Poetry* (see p. 45).

Unable to find work after leaving the Slade in March 1914, and to improve his health, he travelled to South Africa in Spring 1914 to stay with my mother and father. In spite of his family's pleas to remain he returned home once war had been declared later that year. Isaac was against war on principle, but because of the war he was unable to sell any of his work. In desperation he joined the Army. But he was completely unsuitable to be a soldier. He was a dreamer; he was not accustomed to physical effort, so he suffered and often got into trouble. Under the dreadful conditions in the trenches he continued to write poetry and correspond. He wrote to his patron Edward Marsh, 'it's really my being lucky enough to bag an inch of candle that incites me to this pitch of punctual epistolary. I must measure my letter by the light' (CW79, p. 272). The letter is postmarked 2 April 1918, and by the time it arrived, Isaac had already been killed. He had also sent Marsh his last poem:

> Through these pale cold days
> What dark faces burn
> Out of three thousand years,
> And their wild eyes yearn,
>
> While underneath their brows
> Like waifs their spirits grope
> For the pools of Hebron again –
> For Lebanon's summer slope.
>
> They leave these blond still days
> In dust behind their tread
> They see with living eyes
> How long they have been dead.*

---

* See Isaac Rosenberg, *Selected Poems and Letters*, edited and introduced by Jean Liddiard (London: Enitharmon Press, 2003), p. 113 [*SPL*].

When Isaac's father Barnett learned of his son's death, he wrote this lament in his bible. It is in Yiddish, and Isaac's friend Joseph Leftwich translated it:

Day and night I weep, remembering his good crownings.
May the good God have him in mind, his good deeds that he
did in his lifetime.

As it says in Job, the Lord gave and the Lord took away. To praise
his good deeds, let what he left behind be his eternal memory.
With threefold tears I write these verses.

My aunt Annie (Wynick), his elder sister, typed out all the poems that Isaac had sent her from the Front, and kept his manuscripts. She became his literary executor, and laboured tirelessly for years to get recognition for her brother after his death. But it is only in later years that he has gained acceptance as a poet.

Isaac Rosenberg is now held to be one of England's outstanding war poets; his poetry is in every anthology of modern English poetry, and his letters and poetry manuscripts are in the British Library and the Imperial War Museum. His self-portraits may be found in the Tate Gallery and the National Portrait Gallery, while his drawings are held by the British Museum and other paintings by the Imperial War Museum. His name is engraved on a tablet with the names of sixteen war poets in Poets' Corner, Westminster Abbey.

ISAAC HORVITCH
*Isaac Horvitch (1920–2005) was Isaac Rosenberg's
nephew and his literary executor*

Chronology

1890   25 November Isaac Rosenberg born at 5 Adelaide Place, Bristol, eldest son and second child of Barnett (or Barnard) and Anna Rosenberg. Their first child, a daughter Minnie, had been born in Lithuania in 1887. In 1887–8 Barnett had emigrated to England from Lithuania, followed by his wife and child. From Leeds in Yorkshire they moved to Bristol.

1892   Sister Annie born in Bristol.

1894   Sister Rachel born in Bristol.

1897   Brother David born in Bristol.

1897   Family moves to 47 Cable Street, Stepney, London E1. Isaac enrols at St Paul's School, Wellclose Square, St George's in the East.

1899   Brother Elkon born.

1899   14 November. Isaac enrols at Baker Street School, Stepney East.

1900?   Family move to 58 Jubilee Street, Stepney. They become acquainted with the family of John H. Amschewitz (1882–1942), a professional artist who encourages Isaac and introduces him to the schoolteacher Winifreda Seaton (see p. 24). She befriends and corresponds with him until his death. (Winifreda Seaton to Laurence Binyon, p. 129.)

1902   Isaac begins special classes at Stepney Green Art School, sent by his headmaster, who has awarded him a special prize for good conduct. His sister Minnie takes him to meet the librarian of Whitechapel Library, Morley Dainow, when he is about eleven years of age. Dainow introduces him to the major Victorian poets including Dante Gabriel Rossetti, and Rosenberg sends him his early poem 'David's Harp' in September 1905. (Morley Dainow to Binyon, p. 130).

1905   Isaac is apprenticed to Carl Hentschel's, Engravers, of Fleet Street. During this period Isaac meets Frank Emanuel, a painter who invited Isaac to attend a club of artists and art teachers called 'The Limners', who met at his studio 'to bring East and West end together and under the mutual interest of art to foster such social intercourse as would lessen class feeling' (Frank Emanuel to Binyon, p. 127). Emanuel was appointed as Isaac's 'guardian' by the Jewish Board of Guardians who supported his apprenticeship.

1907   Family moves to 159 Oxford Street, London East. Isaac starts evening classes at London School of Photo-engraving and Lithography, Bolt Court, Fleet Street. He continues to frequent the Whitechapel Library and Art Gallery with friends and fellow artists Mark Gertler and David Bomberg.

1908   At Amschewitz's suggestion Isaac attends evening classes at Birkbeck College and is taught by Alice Wright who discusses poetry with him, especially William Blake, and corresponds with him until his death. He is awarded two prizes for his drawing.

1909   Isaac is apprenticed to Lascelles, a process engraver of Shoe Lane in the City of London, still under Hentschel's patronage.

1911   Isaac meets young Jewish writers and artists Samuel Winsten, Joseph Leftwich and John Rodker, who later become established writers, and they form a group centred on the Whitechapel Library and Art Gallery in East London, becoming known as the Whitechapel Boys. By March he has left his work with Hentschel.

1911   17 March. Isaac, copying in the National Gallery, meets Lily Delissa Joseph (sister of the artist Solomon J. Solomon RA); taken on as her son's art tutor, he meets her sister Mrs Henrietta Lowy, and Mrs Herbert Cohen. He paints the self-portrait now in the National Portrait Gallery. In July, still unemployed and depressed, he has a brief holiday in St Helena. Back home he hears that the three ladies will sponsor his attendance at the Slade School of Fine Art in London.

1911   13 October. Isaac joins the Slade School. Mrs Lowy's daughter Ruth is a fellow student (she later marries the publisher Victor Gollancz). His friends Bomberg and Gertler also attend, and other colleagues include C. R. W. Nevinson, Stanley Spencer,

Dora Carrington, Jacob Kramer, William Roberts and Edward Wadsworth.

1912 Isaac writes to and meets the poet Laurence Binyon, curator (eventually Keeper) of Prints and Drawings at the British Museum (see p. 22), who corresponds with him and would write the Introductory Memoir to *Poems by Isaac Rosenberg* (PR22). He receives the Slade School of Arts First Class Certificate for the 1911–12 session.

1912 Spring/summer. Isaac produces 50 copies of his first 24-page pamphlet of poems *Night and Day*, printed for him by his friend Reuben Cohen at Israel Narodiczky in the Mile End Road for £2. In the summer he briefly leases a studio at 32 Carlingford Road, Hampstead.

1912 Winter. Rosenberg family moves to 87 Dempsey Street, Stepney East. In December he rents a room at 1 St George's Square, Regent's Park.

1912 Isaac has disagreements with his patrons and instead receives funds from Jewish Educational Aid Society until he leaves the Slade in 1914. He exhibits two paintings at the New English Arts Club and sells one for £4, enabling him to repay Mrs Herbert Cohen's loan of £2.

1913 Summer. Isaac spends holiday to recover failing health in Sandown, Isle of Wight, accompanied by Whitechapel friend and fellow Slade student, David Bomberg. In August Isaac's sister Minnie marries Wolf Horvitch and the couple leave for South Africa.

1913 November. Mark Gertler introduces Isaac at the Café Royal to the poet T. E. Hulme and to Edward Marsh, private secretary to Winston Churchill and a patron of the arts, who published five volumes of the popular anthology *Georgian Poetry* (see p. 20). Marsh buys Isaac's pictures, writes regularly to him and encourages his poetry.

1914 March. Isaac leaves Slade School of Fine Art.

1914 May. Isaac exhibits at Whitechapel Art Gallery's Exhibition of Twentieth Century Artists.

1914   Isaac, unable to find work and in poor health, gains a grant from the Jewish Educational Aid Society and sails for South Africa to stay with his sister Minnie in Cape Town in 1914. He completes some paintings and gives lectures on art, published with two poems in magazine *South African Women in Council*.

1914   4 August. Great Britain declares war on Germany.

1915   March. Isaac arrives back home in Dempsey Street.

1915   April. Isaac produces 100 copies of his second pamphlet of poems, *Youth*, printed by Israel Narodiczky for £2.10s, paid for by selling three pictures to Edward Marsh.

1915   May. Isaac meets the author Sydney Schiff (pen name Stephen Hudson) at the Café Royal (see p. 23). He reads Isaac's poems and corresponds with him until his death. To Schiff Isaac mentions his play *Moses* for the first time.

1915   June/July/August. *Colour* magazine edited by T. M. Wood prints 'Heart's First Word', 'A Girl's Thoughts' and 'Wedded (1)'. The poet Ezra Pound recommends Isaac's work to Harriet Monroe, editor of the influential magazine *Poetry* (Chicago) (see p. 45).

1915   September. Isaac starts evening classes in block-making, but fails to find work.

1915   October. Isaac enlists and is sent to Recruiting Depot at Bury St Edmunds, Suffolk, to join Bantam Battalion of 12 Suffolk Regiment 40th Division, as he is too short for other units. In November he wrote to Schiff, 'I wanted to join the R.A.M.C. as the idea of killing upsets me a bit, but I was too small.' (To Schiff, November 1915, *CW79*, p. 221.)

1915   November. Isaac is in hospital with cut hands after a fall. Lascelles Abercrombie, poet and critic (see p. 22), starts correspondence with Isaac after his friend Marsh shows him Isaac's poems.

1916   16 January. After four days' Christmas home leave Isaac transfers to 12th South Lancashires, Blackdown Camp, Farnborough, Hants.

1916   March. Isaac transfers again to 11th Battalion King's Own Royal Lancasters at Blackdown Camp as Private Isaac Rosenberg, no. 22311. On 11 March Isaac writes to Abercrombie, 'I send you here my two latest poems, which I have managed to write, though in the utmost distress of mind, or perhaps because of it. Believe me the army is the most detestable invention on this earth and nobody but a private in the army knows what it is to be a slave' (CW79, p. 230). One of the poems was 'Marching'; the other may have been 'Spring 1916'.

1916   19 May. During six days' embarkation leave Reuben Cohen of Narodiczky's (under name of Paragon Printing Works) prints Isaac's last pamphlet of poems and his verse play, *Moses*.

1916   3 June. Isaac embarks with his unit and arrives in France. He writes 'The Troop Ship' describing the embarkation.

1916   June. In mid-June Isaac, at John Rodker's urging, begins a correspondence lasting until his death with two older poets, R. C. Trevelyan, poet and translator from classical literature, and Gordon Bottomley, Georgian poet and dramatist (see p. 22), who was staying with Trevelyan when Isaac's letter arrived. Bottomley encouraged Isaac in life and preserved his reputation and many of his manuscripts after his death, editing and selecting the *Poems* (PR22), and co-editing with D. W. Harding the *Collected Works* (CW37). Isaac's unit of A company is attached to a unit of the Black Watch for training and moves into the trenches in mid-June, in the Hullock section. Isaac begins 'Break of Day in the Trenches'.

1916   1 July. The Somme offensive begins, with heavy casualties. Isaac's 11th K.O.R.L. battalion was part of the 40th Division moved into the line in the Lens area as the preceding divisions were sucked into the offensive. Isaac sends home 'August 1914'.

1916   September. Isaac sends 'Break of Day in the Trenches' to Harriet Monroe of *Poetry* (Chicago).

1916   25 November. Isaac's 26th birthday.

1916   December. Harriet Monroe prints 'Marching' (sent in by John Rodker in January 1916) and 'Break of Day in the Trenches' (sent in by Rosenberg with 'The Troop Ship' in October 1916) in *Poetry* (Chicago).

1917	January. Isaac's health fails and he is assigned to a Works Battalion behind the lines.
1917	Early May. Isaac's health improves and in a letter to Marsh he mentions 'Dead Man's Dump'.
1917	Late May. Isaac writes to Marsh again about 'Dead Man's Dump' and another poem, almost certainly 'Daughters of War', as well as mentioning his play *The Amulet*.
1917	June. Isaac reassigned to 229 Field Company Royal Engineers, attached to 11th Battalion K.O.R.L.
1917	July/August. Isaac writes to Marsh and Bottomley about the drafts of his play, now called *The Unicorn*.
1917	16 September. Isaac at home on leave for ten days; makes contact with Bottomley, Schiff and Trevelyan. He meets scholar and critic Jacob ('Jack') Isaacs at the Café Royal. On his return he is sent back to his battalion.
1917	Late September. *Georgian Poetry* * (third volume, edited by Marsh) published, including extract 'Ah! Koelue!' from Isaac's play *Moses*.
1917	Late October. Isaac admitted to 51st General Hospital with influenza and remains there until December. In a letter to his boyhood friend Leftwich, refers to his two soldier brothers also being in hospital.
1918	Late January. Isaac back in the trenches with 4th Platoon A Company 11th K.O.R.L.
1918	7 February. Isaac transferred to 8th Platoon B Company 1st Battalion K.O.R.L. in the 4th Division, after 11th Battalion broke up owing to shortage of men.
1918	Early March. Isaac writes to Marsh that he has requested a transfer to the Jewish Battalion in Mesopotamia. Isaac manages to meet his brother David.
1918	11 March. Isaac's 1st K.O.R.L. Battalion moves to Arras for training.

---

* *Georgian Poetry* in five volumes, compiled by Edward Marsh, published by Harold Monro (London: The Poetry Bookshop, 1912–22).

1918	19 March. Isaac's battalion moves into front line, the Greenland Hill Sector near Arras, until 24 March.
1918	21 March. The German Army launches its great spring offensive, and the front line has to fall back to Fampoux.
1918	28 March. 1st Battalion K.O.R.L. moves back into front line. Isaac writes his last letter to March enclosing his final poem, 'Through these pale cold days' (Foreword, p. 13). The Germans launch full-scale attack and Isaac's battalion loses seventy men.
1918	31 March. Isaac detailed for a wiring patrol that night.
1918	1 April. Isaac fails to return. His remains are later found with those of his comrades, eleven members of the K.O.R.L., who were buried initially in Northumberland Cemetery, Fampoux.
1919	This cemetery was eventually moved, and Isaac's remains were among the six that could not be individually identified. They were reburied, each with an individual gravestone, in Bailleul Road East British Cemetery, St Laurent Blangy, north east of Arras in Northern France. On Rosenberg's gravestone, below his name, rank, dates and the carved regimental badge of the K.O.R.L., are the following: 'Buried near this spot', the Star of David, and the words 'Artist and Poet'.

Friends and Correspondents of Rosenberg mentioned in the letters

ABERCROMBIE, Lascelles (1881–1938), poet and critic, was a friend of Edward Marsh and a founder member of the 'Georgian' poetry movement in 1912. One of Rosenberg's most admired mentors, he was a friend of Bottomley's, and like him wrote dramatic poems. Unfit for active service during the First World War, he worked as an examiner of munitions in Liverpool. Afterwards he entered academic life and later became Professor of English Literature first at Leeds University, then at Bedford College, London University.

BINYON, Laurence (1869–1943), poet and art historian, worked in the Department of Prints and Drawings at the British Museum, setting up the oriental art collection and becoming Keeper in 1932. In 1915 and 1917 he took leave to volunteer as an orderly in a military hospital in France for some weeks, resulting in his war poem 'Fetching the Wounded', and in 1917 was sent back to France by the Red Cross to report on the work of British volunteers there. His most famous poem however was his 1914 elegy 'For the Fallen', especially its central quatrain beginning 'They shall grow not old, as we that are left grow old'. He was appointed Professor of Poetry at Harvard University from 1933 to 1934. Rosenberg wrote to him in 1912 and was invited to meet him at the British Museum. Binyon helped and encouraged him with his poetry and corresponded with him regularly until Rosenberg's death in 1918. In 1922 he wrote the Introductory Memoir to the selection of *Poems* by Rosenberg (*PR22*).

BOTTOMLEY, Gordon (1874–1948), professional poet and dramatist of the 'Georgian' movement. Because of ill-health Bottomley remained most of his adult life at his home 'The Sheiling' in Silverdale, Lancashire, where he welcomed artists and poets and from there corresponded with them – most notably Edward Thomas and Paul Nash. Although they never met, Rosenberg much admired his work, and from June 1916 Bottomley encouraged and corresponded with him, reading and commenting on his poems until Rosenberg's death in 1918. Bottomley and his literary executors ensured the survival of many of Rosenberg's original manuscripts and drawings. Bottomley selected and edited the first posthumous collection of Rosenberg's *Poems* in 1922 (PR22), and in 1937 collaborated with the critic D. W. Harding on the *Collected Works* (CW37).

MARSH, Edward (later Sir Edward) (1872–1955), patron of the arts and career civil servant, private secretary to Winston Churchill during the First World War. The compiler of five successful volumes of *Georgian Poetry* from 1912 to 1922 (p. 20) and a discerning collector of contemporary works of art, Marsh devoted his small private income to supporting young artists and writers, including many of the 'Whitechapel Boys'. He was Rosenberg's most important and long-standing patron, buying his paintings, including *Sacred Love*, and published an extract from *Moses* in *Georgian Poetry 1916–17* (p. 26). Marsh read and criticized Rosenberg's poems and corresponded with him faithfully until Rosenberg's death in 1918. Rosenberg's last letter and poem were sent to Marsh the day before he died.

ROSENBERG, Annie (1892–1961), Rosenberg's elder sister, later Mrs Wynick, to whom he sent his poems for typing and safekeeping. She became his first literary executor and dedicated herself to promoting his reputation.

SCHIFF, Sydney (1868–1944), Jewish writer, publisher and translator under the pen name Stephen Hudson. Rosenberg met him in spring 1915, and Schiff corresponded with Rosenberg, reading and commenting on his poems, helping him with gifts of money and artist's materials, and sending him newspapers and books once Rosenberg was sent on active service to France.

SEATON, Winifreda, a middle-aged schoolmistress whom Rosenberg met sometime during 1910 in Amschewitz's studio. She encouraged Rosenberg by reading his poems and lending him books to read, introducing him in particular to Donne and the Metaphysical poets. Isaac corresponded with her and continued to send her his poems until his death in 1918.

TREVELYAN, Robert Calverley ('Bob') (1872–1951), prolific poet and translator from Greek and Latin authors, and from June 1916 a correspondent and supporter of Rosenberg's.

Publications and Collections of Manuscripts, Paintings and Drawings

Isaac Rosenberg never had the chance to publish his later poems himself in book form, and it was his mentors Laurence Binyon and Gordon Bottomley, the two correspondents in the following sequence of letters, who were responsible for liaising with his family and friends to assemble the material for the 1922 selection of *Poems* (PR22). Bottomley joined with the critic Denys Harding to produce the 1937 edition of the *Collected Works* (CW37), which went out of print soon afterwards. Its publisher, Ian Parsons of Chatto and Windus, joint literary executor with the poet Patric Dickinson, brought out a new edition in 1979. This too has long been out of print. Now a complete and revised variorum edition of *The Poems and Plays of Isaac Rosenberg* (PPIR), newly edited and introduced by Dr Vivien Noakes (without the letters) has appeared from Oxford University Press in 2004. My own volume, Isaac Rosenberg's *Selected Poems and Letters* (SPL), was published by Enitharmon Press in 2003.

PUBLICATIONS DURING ROSENBERG'S LIFETIME

A Piece of Mosaic, a small private Jewish publication, printed Rosenberg's poem 'In the Workshop' (May 1912).

The Jewish Chronicle printed Rosenberg's review of an exhibition of the work of J. H. Amschewitz and Henry Ospovat, 'Romance at the Baillie Galleries' (24 May 1912).

Night and Day: pamphlet of poems, 24pp, 50 copies printed for Rosenberg by Israel Narodiczky for £2 (1912).

Youth: pamphlet of poems, 100 copies printed for Rosenberg by Israel Narodicszky for £2.10s (April 1915).

South African Women in Council magazine published Rosenberg's lectures on 'Art' and two poems, 'The Dead Heroes' and 'Beauty (II)' (December 1914 and January 1915).

Colour: magazine edited by T. M. Wood, published 'Heart's First Word' (June), 'A Girl's Thoughts' (July) and 'Wedded (I)' (August 1915).

Moses: pamphlet of poems and verse play, printed for Rosenberg by Reuben Cohen of Narodiczky's under name of 'Paragon Printing Works 8 Ocean Street Stepney Green.' Rosenberg offered them for sale to friends at 1s. or cloth bound 4/6d each (May 1916).

Poetry (Chicago) magazine, edited by Harriet Monroe, published 'Marching' and 'Break of Day in the Trenches' (December 1916).

Georgian Poetry 1916–17, volume 3, anthology compiled by Edward Marsh, published by Harold Monro (London: The Poetry Bookshop, September 1917), included 'Ah! Koelue!', extract from Rosenberg's play *Moses*.

PUBLICATIONS AFTER ROSENBERG'S DEATH

Poems and Plays of Isaac Rosenberg, edited by Vivien Noakes (Oxford: Oxford University Press, 2004).

Isaac Rosenberg, *Selected Poems and Letters*, edited and introduced by Jean Liddiard (London: Enitharmon Press, 2003).

Collected Works of Isaac Rosenberg: Poetry, Prose, Letters, Paintings and Drawings, edited with an introduction by Ian Parsons; foreword by Siegfried Sassoon (London: Chatto & Windus, 1979).

Poems by Isaac Rosenberg, edited by Denys Harding (London: Chatto & Windus 1972; paperback 1982).

Collected Works of Isaac Rosenberg: Poetry, Prose, Letters, and Some Drawings, edited by Gordon Bottomley and Denys Harding; foreword by Siegfried Sassoon (London: Chatto & Windus, 1937; reissued as poems and plays only in 1949).

Poems by Isaac Rosenberg, edited by Gordon Bottomley; memoir by Laurence Binyon (London: William Heinemann, 1922).

Art and Letters, edited by Frank Rutter and Osbert Sitwell, published by Sydney Schiff, printed five poems and a pencil study, together with Annie Rosenberg's *Memoir* (Summer 1919, see pp. 133–6).

PUBLIC COLLECTIONS OF MANUSCRIPTS, PAINTINGS AND DRAWINGS

The British Library, London: a collection of poems and letters, including the present newly discovered correspondence and draft poems.

The British Museum Prints and Drawings Department, London: a collection of drawings.

The Imperial War Museum, London: a collection of manuscript poems, letters, paintings and photographs.

The Berg Collection at the New York Public Library: Edward Marsh's collection of correspondence, including Rosenberg's letters to him.

The Slade School of Fine Art, London: some paintings.

Tate Britain and The National Portrait Gallery: each holds a self-portrait by Rosenberg.

FURTHER READING

Jean Liddiard, *Isaac Rosenberg: The Half Used Life* (London: Victor Gollancz, 1975).

Isaac Rosenberg 1890–1918: A Poet and Painter of the First World War, catalogue for the National Book League Exhibition *Word and Image VI*, by Jean Liddiard (London: National Book League, 1975).

Joseph Cohen, *Journey to the Trenches: the Life of Isaac Rosenberg 1890–1918* (London: Robson Books, 1975).

INTRODUCTION

Isaac Rosenberg's newly discovered letters and draft poems

In 1995 the British Library was preparing its great move from the British Museum northwards to its new home near St Pancras Station, and both institutions had of course much sorting out to do. Among the items uncovered was a box containing bundles of letters to Laurence Binyon, including Rosenberg's letters to Binyon and to Gordon Bottomley, still in the large envelope in which Binyon had kept them. It is a mystery why Binyon overlooked them when he retired from his post as Keeper of Prints and Drawings at the British Museum in 1933, as by this stage Gordon Bottomley and the critic Denys Harding would have been thinking about their edition of the *Collected Works* (CW37), eventually published in 1937. However, mislaid they were, and only the extracts and poem versions already published in the 1922 *Poems* (PR22) were reprinted. Also in the bundle were Rosenberg's sister Annie's memoir of her brother, and letters about Rosenberg sent to Binyon by correspondents and mentors of Rosenberg: Morley Dainow, the Librarian of Whitechapel Library, Frank Emanuel, artist, and Winifreda Seaton, schoolteacher.

Isaac Rosenberg has long been regarded as one of the most important artistic figures of the First World War. His poems, such as 'Dead Man's Dump' and 'Break of Day in the Trenches', have been included in every significant war anthology and have earned him a place in Poets' Corner. Yet this reputation was dearly won. After his death he was largely forgotten, and only the devotion of his family and the support of fellow poets rescued his poetry for publication. He was overshadowed by the more acceptably English war poets such as Brooke, Sassoon and Owen, and his poetry did not fit the poetic ideals of the period, just as he, an East End Jew born of immigrant parents, did not present the usual image of the heroic soldier poet which the contemporary public demanded. But the originality and strength of his poetry was rooted in the opposing elements of his life – a life which did not follow the conventions of any role he played: Jew, poet, painter or soldier. For him external circumstances and inward aspiration were continually at odds. He was an immigrant in an alien land, born an orthodox Jew in a Christian culture, a working-class boy with ambitions usually available only to the educated and moneyed classes. He was a Jew who abandoned strict orthodoxy, a painter and poet who grew out of sympathy with the Modernist developments of his time, yet remained a close friend of artists in the forefront of new movements, He came from a traditionally pacifist culture yet became a soldier serving in the most savage of wars. Only in his work did he resolve the conflicts of his fragmented experience, which destroyed his life, but created his poetry.

Born in Bristol in 1890, he moved as a child with his Jewish immigrant family to the East End of London. Here he attended Baker Street School, Stepney from 1899, and was encouraged to pursue his artistic talent, as his sister Annie recalled: 'His headmaster took a special interest in him & allowed him to spend all his time at school in Drawing and writing! Even out of school hours this tendency for drawing would lead young Isaac to become a "pavement artist" in the street, when he would portray several people, much to the amusement and consternation of crowds, which would assemble to watch him' (Annie Wynick, 'In Memory of my Dear Brother', p. 133).

He snatched what time he could for drawing and writing, and from childhood was passionate about both. The young librarian of the Whitechapel Library and Art Gallery, Morley Dainow, remembered their meeting when Rosenberg was under twelve years old: 'One day I was approached by a Jewish lady [Minnie Rosenberg] who asked me whether I could help her young brother whose aim in life was to be a poet. The next day a fragile Jewish boy was brought to me by this lady . . . I took young Rosenberg for walks, and discovered him to be perfectly convinced that his vocation in life was that of a Poet and Painter. I enjoyed being with this boy and was much impressed by his confidence and sensitivity' (Dainow to Binyon, p. 131).

He never lacked confidence in his vocation of art and poetry, and whatever his diffidence in social relations, he was persistent in seeking out either like-minded contemporaries or those, usually older, who could help him as patrons or mentors. He had long frequented the studio of his friend and neighbour, the painter John H. Amschewitz, and there met Winifreda Seaton, a middle-aged schoolteacher who lent him books, introducing him to the Metaphysical poets. They corresponded for the rest of his life. She wrote to Binyon: 'Had he Rupert Brooke's advantages he might have expressed himself more perfectly, but when you compare the environment of the two, Isaac Rosenberg is a wonder . . . He grew to care for Donne almost as much as I do . . . and I remember a note of his beginning "You cruel girl, what have you done with my Donne?" when I kept an old and rather curious copy he picked up somewhere, and was in the habit of looking into every day' (Seaton to Binyon, p. 129).

He was reluctantly obliged to leave school at fourteen and earn his living as an apprentice engraver. During this time he was befriended by his guardian, Frank L. Emanuel, appointed by the Jewish Board of Guardians, who helped support the apprenticeship. Emanuel was a painter and at his studio ran a club for young artists known as 'The Limners', with occasional public exhibitions of their work: 'I felt that it was an opportunity to bring East and West end together and under the mutual interest of art to foster such social intercourse as would lessen class feeling. For Rosenberg whose circumstances had rendered him very bitter and despondent I felt to become a member would be a good thing . . .' (Emanuel to Binyon, p. 127).

Rosenberg would meet his young friends from the Jewish immigrant community, like the painters Mark Gertler, David Bomberg, and the poets Joseph Leftwich and John Rodker, at the Whitechapel Library and Art Gallery in the evenings, and they became known as the Whitechapel Boys. Afterwards they walked the streets discussing art and literature, pausing under lampposts to read their poems. The tedium of his apprenticeship and then the frustration of being out of work with no money drove him all the more to his two art forms, and to reading as widely as he could with the resources of the Library and his mentors. The gulf between the Whitechapel Boys and the older poets, most of whom had received a traditional classical university education, was very great, and these letters burn with Rosenberg's desire to engage with as much literature and art as he could get hold of: the Greeks, Shakespeare and the Elizabethans, the Romantics, the major Victorian poets, and the Authorised Version of the Bible which, as a Jew, he had not read in childhood: 'I read the Sermon on the mount for the first time lately, & got this rare pleasure. It is indeed heroic & great philosophy' (Letter O to Bottomley, p. 94).

Determined to pursue those who could help him, in 1912 he wrote to the poet and art historian Laurence Binyon, working at the Prints and Drawings Department of the British Museum, and encouraged by his reply, wrote again of his interests: 'Amongst modern artists Rossetti appeals very much to me & also his poems. I think his "Beata Beatrix" has as much of the divine insight as any Lippi Lippi [sic] – more I should say, because in it Rossetti has deified a human passion and not as the Italians did humanized deity' (Letter 1 to Binyon, p. 63).

Rosenberg too would engage in his poems and plays with the concept of the 'fierce imaginings' of passionate humanity as a creative force, refusing to be overwhelmed by the divine; this for him always carried William Blake-like connotations of seductive but rapacious power. His last play, The Unicorn, 'is to be a play of terror – terror of hidden things and the fear of the supernatural' (Letter R1 to Bottomley, p. 105).

Binyon invited Rosenberg to meet him at the British Museum, and, as Isaac Horvitch records in his Foreword (p. 12), recalled the meeting some ten years later, struck by the 'independent nature' and determination of the young man, 'with an unusual mixture of self-reliance and modesty' (PR22, pp. 3–5). Like all Rosenberg's friends and correspondents Binyon was sufficiently impressed to act as mentor and correspondent, to look at his work, both written and visual, and to introduce it to friends and professional acquaintances. In May or June of 1912 Rosenberg at his own expense printed his first pamphlet of ten poems, Night and Day.

Thanks to some wealthy Jewish ladies whom he had met whilst drawing in the National Gallery in March 1911, he had been enabled to study from October of that year at the Slade School of Art. He attended together with his friends David Bomberg and Mark Gertler, at the same time as other students of that talented generation, such as Stanley and Gilbert Spencer, C. R. W. Nevinson and Dora Carrington. Like his contemporaries he was excited by the new Post-Impressionist and Modernist ideas in the visual arts flowing across from France, although in his art as in his poetry he never committed himself wholly to any of the lively and usually noisy new experimental groups of young writers and artists. Nonetheless his lady patrons seemed disturbed by what they saw of his work, and he disliked their well-meaning interference. The response of the older generation to the artistic upheavals of the 1900s is exemplified by his earlier patron Frank Emanuel:

> I always regretted that . . . certain of his friends decided to send him to the Slade School – at this time enveloped in an extremely nasty and unhealthy 'atmosphere'. The art produced there was morbid, artificial and unclean and that influence has not yet dissipated itself. The influence was bad for any young artist and doubly so for the already socialistic East End boys, who really required fresh air and sunshine let into their work and their lives to make their lives and achievements healthier and happier. At the Slade stage scenery was preferred to nature, ugliness, sordidness and disease were preferred in its models – to beauty and health and cleanliness.' [Emanuel to Binyon, pp. 127–8]

Rosenberg won a second prize for painting in his first year, and exhibited and sold some work at the New English Art Club Exhibition in October 1913. Following the breach with his lady patrons, the Jewish Educational Aid Society paid his fees until the completion of his course at the Slade in March 1914.

At the Café Royal in Regent Street – a meeting place for the artistic and literary worlds – Mark Gertler introduced Rosenberg to the poet and philosopher T. E. Hulme, and to Edward Marsh, patron of the arts and editor of the *Georgian Poetry* anthologies (p. 20). Marsh became another patron and correspondent of Rosenberg, and bought his paintings and drawings as well as his poetry pamphlets. Much of Rosenberg's work has been dispersed or lost, but his striking series of self-portraits largely survives. He showed promise as a painter but struggled to make a living, and in 1914 he visited his married sister Minnie in South Africa to improve his health and earn some money through painting. He gave some lectures on art which he published with two poems in a women's magazine (p. 25) and undertook one or two commissions, but although he enjoyed the change and the climate he did not find the success he had hoped, and he missed the excitement and stimulus of the London scene. His 1916 character Moses similarly rejects the Africa of the 'Pharaoh well peruked and oiled':

> As ladies' perfumes are
> Obnoxious to stern natures,
> This miasma of a rotting god
> Is to me.
> Who has made of the forest a park?
> Who has changed the wolf to a dog?
>
> And put the horse in harness?
> And man's mind in a groove?*
> [*Moses* 1916, *PPIR*, p. 192]

The 'rotting god' whom Rosenberg constantly challenges in his poetry eventually answered Moses: he replied out of the fire and the whirlwind. And while Rosenberg was still in South Africa in August 1914 war was declared.

In spite of family pressure to stay he felt isolated in South Africa and came home in March 1915, but found it impossible to find work. He printed another pamphlet of his own poems, *Youth,* and paid for the 100 copies by selling three life drawings to Marsh, now Winston Churchill's private secretary at the Admiralty. But the war had changed

London, and the habitués of the Café Royal were scattered; many of his old acquaintances had joined up or were involved in the war effort. In April the war struck closer to home; another protégé of Marsh's, the young poet Rupert Brooke, had been killed on his way to the Dardanelles. Rosenberg had never really cared for Brooke's war poems, 'begloried sonnets' (letter to Mrs Cohen, summer 1916, *CW79*, p. 237) as he called them, but of course wrote to commiserate with Marsh. Marsh was distraught, and found it difficult to give his attention to Rosenberg; as so often the glamour of the dead Brooke put Rosenberg's own achievements in the shade: 'I should not have disturbed you at all but one gets so bewildered in this terrible struggle. Thank you for showing my things to Abercrombie and for thinking of that now' (letter to Edward Marsh, 1915, *CW79*, p. 215).

Lascelles Abercrombie was a poet ten years older than Rosenberg whom the younger man admired very much, especially for Abercrombie's verse plays and his interest in the dramatic aspects of poetry. But he (like Gordon Bottomley and Rupert Brooke) belonged to the centrist Georgian group round Edward Marsh, who wanted to move on from the Victorians but not to break completely with the European humanist tradition; to bring the language of poetry up to date, but not to discard totally traditional forms of verse. At both the Slade and the Café Royal Rosenberg would have been aware of the experimentation with new artistic forms such Futurism and Imagism, enthusiastically promoted by Ezra Pound, T. E. Hulme and Wyndham Lewis, which were also attracting his colleagues in painting and poetry like Gertler, Bomberg, Gaudier-Brzeska and Rodker.

These movements, which were largely just groupings of (usually) quarrelsome individuals, formed and reformed round short-lived little magazines and aimed to subvert the weighty nineteenth-century approach to the arts, now perceived as tired and outdated. Futurism and its home-grown English offshoot, Vorticism, celebrated modern civilization: its noise, its machinery, its speed and its violence. Imagism focused on the importance of clarity, precision of the image and pared-down form in poetry, and T. E. Hulme helped conceive it by making an explicit attack on Romanticism as having corrupted the poets' readership by grandiose, abstract rhetoric: 'verse to them always means a bringing in of some of the emotions that are grouped round the word "infinite".*

Abercrombie and Rosenberg's older mentors of course still held to this traditional view, which Rosenberg himself describes in his first letter to Binyon in 1912 as 'that mysteriousness, the hauntingness which to me is the subtle music' (Letter 1 to Binyon, p. 63). Rosenberg was sure enough of his own vision not to be deterred even by the formidable literary scene of the Café Royal, but what did catch Rosenberg's attention about Hulme's ideas was his way of seeing language as material to be worked with precise, definite techniques: 'Poetry . . . is not a counter language, but a visual concrete one . . . to make you continuously see a physical thing, to prevent you gliding through an abstract process' (Hulme, op. cit., p. 134). Rosenberg was ready to address his own poetic technique to firm up his expression, but he wanted to enlarge, not diminish, his poetic scope – individual lyrics of the Imagist kind seemed to him too thin. His *Youth* was presented in three parts, suggesting some kind of imaginative journey: 'Faith and Fear', 'The Cynic's Lamp' and 'Sunfire'. In 1916, in his second letter to Bottomley, he tries to express what he is aiming at:

> Simple *poetry* – that is where an interesting complexity of thought is kept in tone and right value to the dominating idea so that it is understandable and still ungraspable. I know it is is beyond my reach just now, except, perhaps, in bits. I am always afraid of being empty. When I get more leisure in more settled times I will work on a larger scale and give myself room.' [Letter B to Bottomley, p. 73]

Still unable to find work, he would haunt the Whitechapel Library to read, work on his poems, and meet his old friends. Like all young men at that time they were feeling the pressure of popular expectations. When war had become a normal element of everyday life it was more difficult to stay out of the Armed Forces than to join up. Several

---

* T. E. Hulme, *Speculations* (London: Keegan Paul Trench Trubner, 1936), pp. 126–7.

of them, including John Rodker and Mark Gertler, felt that they had to make a choice between their deep Jewish pacifist beliefs and wartime demands. They publicly opted for pacifism – not an easy choice in 1915 – and Rodker was in fact imprisoned as a conscientious objector. At the Café Royal in May of that year Rosenberg met an older writer, Jewish, cultivated and successful, Sydney Schiff, who became another lifelong correspondent. He gave Schiff a copy of *Youth*; Schiff bought more, and also lent him money to pay for a course in preparing blocks for the printing press as well as encouraging him to keep writing. Rosenberg could express his anxieties about the war to Schiff:

> I am thinking of enlisting if they will have me, though it is against all my principles of justice – though I would be doing the most criminal thing a man can do – I am so sure my mother would not stand the shock that I don't know what to do. [Letter to Schiff, 8 June 1915, *CW79*, p. 216]

Suddenly, in late October, Rosenberg disappeared – neither family or friends knew where he was. Then Schiff received a letter from Private Isaac Rosenberg of the 12th Suffolk Bantams: 'I could not get the work I thought I might so I have joined this Bantam Battalion (as I was too short for any other) which seems to be the most rascally affair in the world . . . besides my being a Jew makes it bad amongst these wretches' (letter to Schiff, October 1915, *CW79*, p. 219).

Rosenberg's poem 'The Jew' has been hitherto dated to this time, but is most likely later, as the pencil draft Poem O is enclosed with Letter O to Bottomley postmarked 11 July 1917 (see pp. 95–6). Yet this merely confirms that he encountered these attitudes throughout his army career:

> The blonde, the bronze skinned & ruddy
> With the same heaving blood
> Keep tide to the moon of Moses
> Yet why do they sneer at me?
>
> [Poem O, p. 96]

His physical fragility added to the endemic discomforts of army life. He wrote from military hospital in December 1915 to Edward Marsh with an appeal to sort out an army bureaucratic muddle, prefaced by a statement of his own ambiguous attitude to the war: contempt for its barbarity, yet acceptance of the inevitable 'trouble' of human existence:

> I never joined the army from patriotic reasons. Nothing can justify war. I suppose we must all fight to get the trouble over . . . I thought if I'd join there would be the separation allowance for my mother. At Whitehall it was fixed up that 16/6d would be given including the 3/6d a week deducted from my 7/-. Its [sic] now between 2 & 3 months since I joined; my 3/6d is deducted right enough, but my mother hasn't received a farthing . . .
> [Letter to Marsh, December 1915, CW79, p. 227]

The Bantam Battalion was broken up as unfit, and Rosenberg eventually ended up in the King's Own Royal Lancasters, as Private 22311. In the late spring of 1916, before his battalion was due to be sent overseas, he came home on leave to visit his mother and to see through the press his final pamphlet of poems, *Moses*. In the final week of May 1916, at John Rodker's suggestion, he sent copies of *Moses* to the poet and translator Robert Calverley Trevelyan: 'I am enclosing one for you and one for Mr Bottomley who is the most real poet living in England' (letter to Trevelyan, May 1916, CW79, pp. 233–4).

Rosenberg's division embarked for France on 2 June 1916. On 1 July the British began the Somme Offensive, and further north Rosenberg's 40th Division took the place in the Lens area of the divisions who were being sucked into the battle. On 4 July 1916 Bottomley, having seen both *Youth* and *Moses*, wrote to Rosenberg for the first time, 'there is no doubt there was never a more real poet in the world than you are'.* This was just what Rosenberg needed to hear, as he began his service on the Western Front. During the summer the battalion was in the trenches for eight days or more, if, as usual, reserves were short. They were then relieved and sent behind the lines for a rest period of up to

* Letter in Marsh Letter Collection in the Berg Collection, New York Public Library.

a week. In really bad winter conditions the front line period was usually reduced to four days. As Rosenberg makes clear, the Army ensured that even in rest periods the men were always kept busy, which meant very little time to themselves, and for him, scarcely time to scribble a letter or draft a verse. Gradually the division moved inexorably southwards towards the Somme; in October it moved to Abbeville for training, and after Christmas 1916 the 11th K.O.R.L. fetched up just south of Bapaume.

Typically of Rosenberg, the bundle of letters and draft poems are written largely in pencil, in haste, – 'I scrawl abominably' – (Letter C to Bottomley, p. 80), and on whatever paper he could get hold of. Among the usual constraints of life as a private soldier on the Western Front there were additional problems for a poet like Rosenberg. Lack of free time was one: 'You know how impossible it is to work it [his poem] out, placed as I am – if I had been an officer, I might have managed it, but we Tommies are too full up' (Letter R3 to Bottomley, pp. 107–8).

Another was finding paper, pencil and light to read and write by: 'I shan't say I don't get the time to read, but when we've done our days [sic] work & get under the tent; [sic] (we are in tents just now) it is dark and lights are not easy to get out here' (Letter J to Bottomley, p. 89). A third was the irksome inability to keep books and papers together, as private soldiers had to carry everything in their packs. The letters are full of requests to his correspondents to keep draft poems for him and not to send him cloth-bound books, much as he longs for them, as he always loses them when his unit shifts about the trenches: 'in fact at any time I prefer cheap bound books I can spoil by reading anywhere. I often find bibles in dead mens clothes [sic] & I tear the parts out I want and carry them round with me' (Letter D to Bottomley, p. 81).

To a young man whose intellectual appetite for books was so great the lack must have been especially infuriating, especially as his urge to fill the gaps in his knowledge emerges so strongly in these letters: 'I have not read the "Chronicles of Jeremiah" & thank you for putting me on it. We Jews are all taught Hebrew in our childhood but I was a young rebel and would not be taught, unluckily now' (Letter O to

Bottomley, p. 95). The letters pulse with Rosenberg's longing for time and opportunity to read more, to write more, and to talk about it all with like-minded friends: 'A friend sent me Swinburne out here & Whitman. . . . Swinburne writes too much for the ladies' (Letter D to Bottomley, p. 81). The freshness of perception that makes his comments so vivid comes out particularly in these letters: 'what I've read have been very few of the Greeks; I have read some of the great dramas, but have always felt (except in Shelley's) the translator use his English in a foreign unnatural empty way, not like the bible translators'. There is also the terse humour he develops against the discomforts of trench life: 'I wonder if Aeschylus as a private in the army was bothered as I am by lice . . .' (Letter J to Bottomley, p. 89).

Yet the fierce commitment to his writing which so struck his family and friends persisted against all the odds, and is caught in these scraps of paper, scrawled by Rosenberg from a trench firestep or a campfire behind the lines. These letters to Binyon and Bottomley pour out his thoughts and his poems in a creative surge; no wonder the older poets responded regularly with appreciation and criticism – both seized upon hungrily by Rosenberg: 'We are fearfully busy now & it has been an effort to write this letter, but your letters always give me great delight, and I must let you know' (Letter R1 to Bottomley, p. 105).

These letters emphasise the peculiar hardship for Rosenberg of not only being away from home in a physically harsh and dangerous world, but also being cut off from the creative activity and interchange with like-minded friends and mentors. Other poets like Siegfried Sassoon, Robert Graves, Wilfred Owen and Edward Thomas also experienced these inhibiting conditions in the trenches, but they were all officers; they may not have had privacy but they had a bed in a dugout, paper and light to write by. They also got better food. An officer would go out in charge of patrols or working parties but he would not himself have to dig latrines from heavy mud or stack railway sleepers hour after hour in the cold. Nor was he subject to punishments for petty infringements. Nor did he have to face the sometimes crude hostility of fellow soldiers to someone not physically strong, a Londoner and Jew (in a Lancashire regiment), whose mind was on other matters and who was consequently not an efficient soldier. It was precisely because Rosenberg could not be fitted into the functional role of the soldier, because he did stubbornly retain his own sense of priorities and kept faith with the poetry welling up constantly in his imagination, that he remained a poet against such heavy odds. The letters were a lifeline to Rosenberg, a link with a happier, more fruitful life where he was not always judged by externals: 'Your letter came to today with Mr Trevelyan's, like two friends to take me for a picnic. Or rather like friends come to release the convict from his chains with his innocence in their hands, as one sees in the twopenny picture palace. You might say, friends come to take you to church, or the priest to the prisoner' (Letter B to Bottomley, p. 73).

With the same letter he encloses a poem, 'In the Trenches' (Poem B, pp. 74–5), a version of what was to become 'Break of Day in the Trenches'. (For the final version see Appendix, pp. 137–8.) This contains some previously unknown final lines, and shows how Rosenberg is taking up the direct and literal elements of the battlefield – the 'poppy' and the 'rat'– and refocusing on the image, learning to strip it down as his Imagist friend Rodker might, yet working for that lucidity not to eliminate mystery, but to evoke it more fully – 'understandable and still ungraspable' (Letter B to Bottomley, p. 73). In the unknown variant Poem B Rosenberg tries out 'poppy blooded fields' instead of the 'sleeping green' crossed by the rat in the familiar final version, and also hails the rat as 'Droll subterranean' which he loses from the final version. The last eight lines from line 19 of the final version read:

> What do you see in our eyes
> At the shrieking iron and flame
> Hurl'd through still heavens?
> What quaver – what heart aghast?
> Poppies whose roots are in man's veins
> Drop and are ever dropping,
> But mine in my ear is safe –
> Just a little white with the dust.

['Break of Day in the Trenches', final version, Appendix, pp. 137–8]

The variant version is much less developed at this stage:

> What do you see in our eyes
> At the hiss, the irrevocable swiftness,
> <As> The laconic earth buffet.
> A shell!
> Safe. Again murder has overlooked us
> Only white with powder and chalk.
> [Poem B, p. 75]

In the accompanying Letter B he tells Bottomley he has already rethought the poem and asked his sister Annie to send Bottomley her typescript. (This is probably the version with punctuation and typing errors corrected in Bottomley's hand now in the Imperial War Museum, cited in *PPIR*.) In this typescript the lines have become:

> What do you see in our eyes
> At the boom, the hiss, the swiftness,
> The irrevocable earth buffet . . .
> What rootless poppies dropping –
> But mine in my ear is safe
> Just a little white with the dust.
> [IR/1237 TS 1, see *PPIR*, pp. 128 & 359]

Still in the same Letter B Rosenberg explains his thinking to Bottomley:

> The poem 'In the Trenches' I altered a little and have asked my sister to send on to you. I left a line out 'a shell's haphazard fury' after 'irrevocable earth buffet'. I don't think I make my meaning quite clear that it is a shell bursting which has only covered my [sic] & the poppy I plucked at the beginning of the poem still in my ear with dust'. [Letter B to Bottomley, p. 73]

Poem B's last lines 'A shell!/Safe . . . seem more like jottings for the images he wants to close the poem. In his typescript version he

42

removes the poppy from the 'blooded field' in line 15 of Poem B (p. 75) – 'To cross the poppy blooded field between' – and returns it to the last four lines: 'rootless poppies dropping'. But in the earlier Poem B it hasn't yet arrived there to pre-empt the too-explicit 'murder' and badge the poem's finale with its now implicit blood colour. Rosenberg's robust poetic imagination refused to settle for less – 'I am always afraid of being empty' – as he transforms those lines into their final version. In Poem B he combines an impression with an explanation: 'A shell!/ Safe. Again murder has overlooked us / Only white with powder and chalk.' But already the phrasing of the final version,* with its pared-down detail, is in Rosenberg's mind – '& the poppy I plucked at the beginning of the poem still in my ear with dust.' In the final version the emphatic 'poppy blooded' of Poem B becomes the suggestive 'roots are in man's veins', and Rosenberg compresses the over-literal 'powder and chalk' of Poem B to bleach the poppy's conventional blood colour into the 'white . . . dust' of mortality, that so tellingly unites the survivor, the dead and the poppy into a brief moment of intense awareness; the effect is enriched by the sensuousness of his painter's eye for the subtle interactions between red and white.

Further on in the same letter he is already considering how to develop this lyric intensity into a larger structure. 'In the Trenches', he goes on, 'is one of a sequence of war poems I want to write', and there follows a vigorous description of himself, his comrades and a group of Scots soldiers hunting fleas the previous night: 'all stripped by candlelight some Scots dancing over the candle & burning the fleas, & the funniest, drollest and dirtiest scenes of conversation ever imagined [sic] . . . 'I have heaps of material' (Letter B to Bottomley, p. 73).

The fleas eventually emerge in two poems: 'The Immortals' and 'Louse Hunting' (*PPIR*, op. cit., pp. 133–4), but he is also thinking of drawing and painting; in September he mentions it to Bottomley: 'I must draw the Flea Hunt if I don't write it but so far Ive [sic] not been able to do anything interesting' (Letter G to Bottomley, p. 84). He eventually produced a sketch and a draft of 'Louse Hunt' the following

---

* 'Break of Day in the Trenches', final version, Appendix, pp. 137–8.

43

February 1917 which he sent to Bottomley. The older poet's characteristically warm response to this also referred to Rosenberg's first description of the scene above:

> I should like to see what you would make of the active Flea-Hunt which you first described, with the men jumping over candles and singeing the fleas. That would yield quite a different kind of composition, all moving and flowing lines, like a Sabbath of long slim bodies as if Botticelli had gone mad and designed a naked ballet for the Russian dancers. And it would be as much your own as the other, for it is all summarised in your letter of last summer.' [Bottomley to Rosenberg, 19 March 1917, IWM/IR/V 17]*

Rosenberg replies in a letter postmarked 8 April 1917: 'I thought you would like the Flea Hunt, and your way of commenting on it is infinitely more superior to my sketch' (Letter L to Bottomley, p. 91). The care with which Bottomley comments on Rosenberg's work (and the consistency of his letters) explain the reciprocated admiration which Rosenberg expresses throughout his correspondence: 'Your letters always give me a strange and large pleasure; and I shall never think I have written poetry in vain, since it has brought your friendliness in my way. Now, feeling as I am, castaway and used up, you don't know what a letter like yours is to me' (Letter K to Bottomley, pp. 89–90).

It was the respect for his work as much as the attention which Bottomley and Binyon accorded Rosenberg that meant so much to him. Subsequent twentieth-century readers and critics of Rosenberg have tended to deplore the effect of the older poets' post-Romantic poetry on Rosenberg's work; this is largely because the rising of the radical Modernist tide, channelled by the First World War, swept all before it, including the last remnants of the traditional poetic goals of 'beauty' and the metaphysical, as well as the traditional technical methods of versification and style. Its energies were ably harnessed by the two non-combatant Americans, Ezra Pound and T. S. Eliot, whose

---

* This and other letters from Bottomley in the Imperial War Museum (IWM), quoted by Vivien Noakes in *PPIR*.

44

own work entirely redefined and dominated the aims and expression of poetry and criticism. For most of the twentieth-century any poet (or critic) whose work did not fit the canons of the new Modernism tended to be relegated, and this fate befell most of Rosenberg's Georgian mentors.

Rosenberg himself was not modishly avant-garde, as Ezra Pound with his Imagist experiments certainly was, although as has been demonstrated Rosenberg was aware of them and learned from them. He probably had more in common with the poet he called 'the established great man', W. B. Yeats, who was also in his education and his interests an outsider on the London literary scene, and who was developing his own poetic world centred on the mythology of Ireland, rather as Rosenberg was also working towards his own mythical structure in which to place and comprehend his personal experience. Yeats met Rosenberg in the winter of 1914–15, and was sufficiently struck by him to draw him to the attention of Ezra Pound. Pound recommended *Youth* to his friend Harriet Monroe, publisher of the influential literary magazine *Poetry* (Chicago): 'I think you may as well give this poor devil a show. Yeats called him to my attention last winter, but I have waited. I think you might do a half a page review of his book, and that he is worth a page for verse . . . He has something in him, horribly rough but then "Stepney", East . . . we ought to have a real burglar . . . ma che!!!'.* (Harriet Monroe eventually printed 'Break of Day in the Trenches' and 'Marching' in December 1916, as Rosenberg tells Binyon in Letter 6, p. 68.)

The Georgian poets however offered Rosenberg what the more intimidating and glamorous Pound and Yeats could not: a steady and informed audience for his poems, so that he had the confidence both to send them work in progress, and to keep writing under the most unpropitious circumstances. Especially important at this point for Rosenberg was the success of Bottomley, Binyon and Abercrombie as playwrights whose verse plays had been both published and performed, even though their work did not fit the canons of the new

---

* Pound to Monroe, August 1915, University of Chicago Library, quoted by Joseph Cohen, *Journey to the Trenches* (London: Robson Books 1975), p. 121.

Modernism. The attempt to revive the medium of the verse drama continued with varying degrees of success throughout the nineteenth and first half of the twentieth century. Although the form has largely been dismissed by modern critics it was taken seriously by most poets from the Romantics onwards. Theatre after all was still the most powerful dramatic medium, as film was still in its infancy. At this period W. B. Yeats was achieving some stir with his own work for Dublin's Abbey Theatre, as Rosenberg commented to Bottomley: 'If we had a theatre as you suggest I believe we would get the great age of poetry back again. I thought Yeats had started something of the kind – the theatre I mean, not the great age' (Letter E to Bottomley, p. 82).

Paradoxically the greatest success of the medium would be *Murder in the Cathedral*, by the arch-Modernist T. S. Eliot. So Rosenberg was not being eccentric by printing his own first attempt at a verse play, *Moses*, and throughout the following letters he is thinking about his next one. He had been exploring the possibility of writing about Judas Maccabeus, the Jewish warrior hero who fought the Romans, remarking to Bottomley: 'Judas as a character is more magnanimous than Moses, and I believe I could make it very intense and write a lot from material out here' (Letter K to Bottomley, p. 90). Bottomley's enthusiasm for Rosenberg's ideas and for his ambition to enlarge the scope of his poetry came promptly back in a letter of 12 February:

> Your idea of doing a Judas Maccabeus is first-rate, and I hope you will keep tight hold of it until you find an opportunity to tackle it. It, and a whole host of the similar gorgeous subjects which are your birthright, have never been properly done in English literature, and I believe you have the power in you to make them your own and make memorable things of them. [IWM IR/V/16]

This was just what Rosenberg needed to hear, and he explores the idea in characteristically unconventional directions in his letter to Binyon: 'I have much real material here, and also there is some parrallel [sic] in the savagery of the invaders then to this war . . . the period is about Christ's time I think I could bring about a meeting between

46

Christ & Judas, in fact Christ could be brought up or spend part of his boyhood with Mathias the High priest [sic] or father of Judas' (Letter 4 to Binyon, p. 66).

Without the time to start writing or the opportunity to research the subject he could not proceed, and turned back to creating his own myth. The fragments he managed to produce suggest that he was attempting to work out his own vision of a world in which the old creeds are broken and in flux through great upheaval, from which something new, on a grander scale than the old drab life, must emerge. This theme is taken up in his last ambitious war poems. He told Bottomley that 'Daughters of War' (of which there are varying draft versions in the following collection) 'came when I was brooding over Judas Maccabeus, it is all that did come of it. If I get back all right, Judas will come too, & all I have learnt our here will be crammed into it' (Letter J to Bottomley, p. 88).

Rather typically, Rosenberg appears to have sent out on the same day two different versions, each 27 lines long – to Bottomley (Poem I, pp. 87–8) and to Binyon (Poem 5, pp. 67–8). Both are postmarked 5 December 1916. He worked on the poem throughout the spring and summer of 1917, and in late July Bottomley had received Annie Rosenberg's typescript of the full text to date (Typescript P, pp. 97–9). In August Rosenberg opened his letter to Bottomley with a revision of the first seven lines, hoping that 'it makes the poem clearer'. He is anxious that Edward Marsh should publish 'Daughters of War' in the third volume of *Georgian Poetry 1916–17*, instead of his brief lyric 'Koelue' from *Moses*: '. . . I am certain my most epic poem, so far, is the Daughters poem, but it is too obscure, he thinks. I believe if one gets hold of the opening it should be easy enough to follow. Where do you think the poem is obscure [sic]' (Letter Qa to Bottomley, pp. 103–4). But to his disappointment Marsh preferred 'Koelue'. However Rosenberg must have been cheered by Bottomley's sympathetic critique of 7 August – 'It is your most remarkable poem for vision and originality and texture of language' (IWM/IR/V/20).

That summer Rosenberg and his imagination were reviving after the harsh winter, during May camping in woods behind the lines: 'it is that I've had a little more time in the day to myself & am with a small loading party by ourselves that I've been able to write these two things'. The current of poetry that always seems to flow through his sensibility wells up once more, refreshing the most squalid and tedious of army tasks. He continues to Bottomley:

> I am now with the Royal Engineers & we go wiring up the line at night . . . I wrote a poem about some dead Germans lying in a sunken road where we dumped our wire. I have asked my sister to send it on to you, though I think it commonplace; also Daughters of War which I've improved. [Letter M to Bottomley, p. 92]

Annie Rosenberg's typescripts of 'Daughters of War' and 'Dead Man's Dump', dated by her May 1917, are enclosed with Letter P, postmarked 23 July 1917 (p. 96), but must have been received earlier in June, as on 29 June Bottomley writes to Rosenberg of 'Dead Man's Dump': 'in places it suggests that it has absorbed more raw material "neat", than it can assimilate. But in places it gets beyond that more completely than any other war poetry I have seen. This kind of quality is your high water mark yet, so you must keep it up' (IWM/IR/V/19). The reaction against the 'raw material' of the battlefield was shared by all the older Georgian poets and by their editor Edward Marsh. Such a break with lyric poetry and the traditional poetic conventions was unacceptable to the latter. Bottomley, as a practising dramatic poet, was more sympathetic to Rosenberg's attempts to reinvent his own poetry and mix free and formal rhythms in 'Dead Man's Dump' than was Marsh. As early as August 1916 Rosenberg had tried to make Marsh understand that for him poetry was organic, not a matter for arbitrary decision. New conditions of life would inevitably create a different poetry to reflect it:

> You know the conditions I have always worked under, and particularly with this last lot of poems. You know how earnestly one must wait on ideas, (you cannot coax real ones to you) and let as it were a skin grow naturally round and through them. If you are not free, you can only, when the ideas come hot, seize

them with the skin in tatters raw, crude, in some parts beautiful in others monstrous. Why print it then? Because these rare parts must not be lost. I work more and more as I write into more depth and lucidity, I am sure. [Letter to Edward Marsh, 4 August 1916, CW 79, p. 239]

The various drafts in the following collection show how determined he was to keep trying. Typescript P of 'Dead Man's Dump' seems to be the same as two (TSS. 3 & 4) in the Imperial War Museum collection; all three include the same lines omitted in the final version (Appendix, pp. 142–4). However also included with Typescript P is an unknown variant of six lines, scribbled by Rosenberg in pencil on a torn scrap of paper. Here he is wrestling with the notion of the sudden wrenching of the 'dark souls' from the corpses, how the living human being with its capacity to encompass and challenge the universe becomes in a violent instant detritus – 'soul's sack'. Typescript P has:

> What fierce imaginings their dark souls lit
> Earth! Have they gone into you?
> Somewhere they must have gone,
> And flung on your hard back
> Is their soul's sack
> Emptied of all that made it more than the world
> In its small fleshly compass.

Dissatisfied with that as too simply descriptive, Rosenberg tries again to rework the last image on his scrap of paper:

> And flung on your hard back
> Is their soul's sack
> Emptied of all that made the young lean Time
> Eye with thief's eyes, shouldering his masters load
> Of proud Godhead ancestralled essences
> Who hurled them out? Who hurled?
>
> [Fragment P, p. 103]

The thief 'Time' seems to have crept in from Shakespeare's *Troilus and Cressida* ('Time hath my lord, a wallet at his back / Wherein he puts alms for oblivion', Act 3, scene 3). Rosenberg next discards 'Time'– possibly as an image too far – but with 'Godhead ancestralled essences' he knew he had struck gold. The final version (Appendix, pp. 142–3) tightens to three lines, the final rich image achieved in just five words:

> And flung on your hard back
> Is their soul's sack
> Emptied of God-ancestralled essences.

Rosenberg is not satisfied with simply reporting the horrors of the battlefield, 'shilling shockers' as he called them in a letter (to R. C. Trevelyan, June 1916, CW79, p. 235). Nor was the evocation of a moment with its pity and horror ('War and the pity of War' as Wilfred Owen had described it) adequate for him. Rosenberg's ambition was to bring to bear on the immediate physical experience of the trenches his insights into the wider nature of creative and destructive power. The frantic activity of the battlefield is measured against the ageless power of earth and nature, which in this as all his war poems is infused with seductive but dangerous devouring power; the other war poets (and the Georgians) like Owen, Edmund Blunden and Edward Thomas, still hold to the Romantic view of a beautiful natural universe, quickened with spiritual power shared by man. Rosenberg stands aside from this tradition, as is shown by his deletion from the final version (pp. 142–4) of four lines from the third stanza of Typescript P, evoking the seasonal cycle of death and rebirth:

> Now let the seasons know
> There are some less to feed of them,
> That Winter need not hoard her snow,
> Nor Autumn her fruits and grain.
> [Typescript P, lines 20–4, p. 100]

For Rosenberg, humanity with its 'fierce imaginings' is central, and he asserts the human value of the destroyed life, not, like Owen, by mourning the beauty of men deformed by death, but characteristically by celebrating the energy of 'their dark souls'.

During that last summer he did not shut out the strain of war, deliberately dull his responses to it as many did to get themselves through it, but made the war and its effect on him serve his own purposes as a poet. The price for a private soldier was sometimes high. He told Bottomley that forgetting his gas-helmet resulted in seven days' pack drill 'which I do between the hours of going up the line and sleep' (Letter N, July–August 1917, p. 93). These were precious hours when he could have been writing, and he felt he still had so much to do:

> I don't suppose my poems will ever be <u>poetry</u> right and proper until I shall be able to settle down and whip myself into more expression. As it is, my not being able to get poetry out of my head & heart causes me sufficient trouble out here. Not that it interferes with the actual practical work; but with forms and things I continually forget, & authority looks at [sic] from a different angle and perspective. [Letter O, pp. 94–5]

In late September 1917, he returned home to Dempsey Street for his last ten days' leave, telling Bottomley that he felt 'restless here and unanchored'; this was an experience he shared with many soldiers returning from the Front. His younger brother David and his brother-in-law are also home on leave: 'and all my people are pretty lively & won't let me isolate myself to write.' However he sorts out some drafts of his play *The Unicorn* to send Bottomley: 'tell me if it appears trashy; I have no feeling about it just now' (Letter R2, p. 106). Delighted by Bottomley's reply he tells him he plans to send him his drawing of 'Adam and Eve' when he can find it, and meanwhile sends him a photograph of himself and his brother (see p. 109): 'I hope you will be ammused [sic] at these things enclosed. . . .The chap with me is my very young brother [David] and I am in civvies again. The suit & the hat is the family suit & hat & fits us all [sic], though my younger brother is growing out of it now' (Letter R3 to Bottomley, p. 107).

On his return to his battalion at the Front in October 1917 he is taken ill again with the influenza sweeping across Europe, and in hospital for most of the rest of the year. This enforced rest at least gave him time to reread Bottomley's poems and think uninterruptedly about his own poetry. He sent Bottomley a draft of 'Girl to Soldier on Leave' (Poem S,

p. 111) which he had roughed out at home, and also 'In War' (Poem T, p. 113), a poem about loss and grief. The story it tells is of a soldier from a burial party who recognised one of the corpses as his own brother. Until now it has not been certain whether it was based on an actual incident, but it is clear from the accompanying letter that it was: 'I enclose a poem Ive [sic] just written – its [sic] sad enough I know – but one can hardly write a war poem & be anything else. It happened to one of our chaps poor fellow – and I've tried to write it' (Letter T, p. 112).

It starts off with two stanzas ('fret the nonchalant noon'), which are preserved in the first fragment (Poem A, p. 72) enclosed with his letter to Bottomley of July 1916 (Letter A, p. 73), showing that it was Rosenberg's practice to keep all his verse jottings for later use. In November 1917 the third *Georgian Poetry 1916–1917* was published and Rosenberg received a copy from Edward Marsh in December.

Out of hospital in January 1918 he told Bottomley he had to send the book back home but had 'just time to gallop through it . . . Im [sic] writing this in the line & have no light or paper' (Letter V to Bottomley, p. 117). By February he found himself caught up in the confusion caused by casualties to his old battalion. He was transferred to the 1st Battalion and moved to Arras: 'my own Batt is broken up & what was left of them mixed up with other Battalions. Just now we are out for a "rest". Poetry seems to have gone right out of me I get no chance to even think of it [sic]' (Letter W to Bottomley, p. 118). In his penultimate letter to Bottomley on 24 February it is clear that he had no chance to write under pressure of the move: 'No drug could be more stupefying than our work (to me anyway) and this goes on like that old torture of water trickling, drop by drop unendingly on one's helplessness . . . I find I can't copy these bits from the Unicorn so am sending one or two poor things, but I aimed for something in them' (Letter X, p. 119). Enclosed in the envelope were holographs of 'The Tower of Sculls' (sic), 'The dying soldier', 'The Burning of the Temple' and a typescript of 'Returning, we hear the larks' (Poem X, pp. 119–22).

Since July 1916 he had had a 'sequence of dramatic war poems' in mind (Letter B, p. 73). In autumn 1916 he mentioned it to Binyon (Letter 4, p. 66) and in December 1916 also to Binyon he spoke of receiving Wilfrid Wilson Gibson's 1916 book of war poems, *Battle*: 'most of the poems are really fine and absolutely express the thing. "Between the Lines" is most vivid & exact. I was never very fond of Gibson's work, it struck me as cultured vigour – but I was delighted with this book' (Letter 5, p. 67).

Gibson's 'Between the Lines', about a soldier stranded in No Man's Land, is echoed in both 'Break of Day in the Trenches' and 'Dead Man's Dump'. But it is Gibson's 'The Lark' that offered Rosenberg the approach that would transform the rather obvious image of the larks above the battlefield into something more resonant. In Gibson's poem Rosenberg found the following:

> A lull in the racket and brattle
> And a lark soars into the light –
> And its song seems the voice of the light
> Quelling the voices of night . . .
> . . . and he drops from the height
> Dead as a stone from the height –
>> ['The Lark', from *Battle* by W. W. Gibson,
>> London: Elkin Mathews, 1916, p. 26]

For Rosenberg in 'Returning, we hear the larks' (Appendix, p. 150) the night is not overcome by light – he reverses that traditional image:

> Sombre the night is,
> And though we have our lives, we know
> What sinister threat lurks there . . .
>
> But hark! joy – joy, strange joy,
> Lo! heights of night ringing with unseen larks
> Music showering our upturned list'ning faces.
>
> Death could drop from the dark
> As easily as song . . .

The soldiers are, like the dreaming man, blind, the larks unseen; the longed-for 'joy' can be apprehended only in darkness and danger, like the girl's 'dark hair' and kisses, but the blackness is nonetheless transfigured aurally by the larksong in the climactic line which echoes Gibson –'Lo! heights of night ringing with unseen larks'. So potent is it that it becomes tangible as falling water, 'showering' on the men, held fast momentarily in spite of the danger by their longing, emphasised by the wave-like cadence of the long/short last four lines with its 'dangerous tides', reminiscent of Keats's 'perilous seas' in 'Ode to a Nightingale'. The delicate movement between sight – or lack of it – and sound, the reversing of the usual Romantic link between lark and light, transfigure the poem by subverting the traditional affirmation of the lark image (which even Gibson keeps), creating a kind of inverted pastoral to which, however, the human experience, not the natural world, is central. The human is always at the heart of Rosenberg's poetry, the acutely observed physical body and its sensations, its vulnerability only emphasising the sharp awareness of the aspiring consciousness, 'list'ning faces'. The poem's conflicting tensions, its intense awareness of a particular moment, the recognition of the inextricable blending of danger and beauty, of which war is only one aspect, charge the poem with a power that, as always with Rosenberg, reaches beyond the immediate context of the battlefield. It shows too how freely his imagination now dominated and used every part of his experience.

On 7 March 1918 Rosenberg wrote his last letter to Bottomley under pressure, knowing they were about to go up the line again. He acknowledges that 'death . . . seems to underlie even our underthoughts', but there is always an indomitable quality to Rosenberg; he is delighted with Bottomley's response to his work: 'your six horse metaphor is very kind & gratifying criticism & you may be sure I will keep it in mind'. He is thinking ahead, hoping for a transfer to 'the Judaens' (the Jewish Battalion in Mesopotamia), to join his friend, the sculptor Jacob Epstein, and looking forward to meeting Bottomley one day and 'the great peacetime pleasure' of reading one of his plays (Letter Y, pp. 122–3). On 19 March the 1st Battalion moved into the line, the Greenland Hill sector near Arras. On 28 March the Germans launched their full scale attack, and the battalion lost seventy men. On the night of 31 March Rosenberg was detailed for a patrol to repair wire in front of the trenches. The patrol never returned. His body was eventually interred with eleven of his comrades in Bailleul Road East British Cemetery, near Arras.

Rosenberg never took the easy way out in his life or his poetry. His later editor, the critic Denys Harding, noted this as a creative strength: 'something in Rosenberg always responded to the challenge of the monstrous misery and threat that war produced; he never *merely* suffered it'.* This is perhaps one answer to W. B. Yeats's famous rejection of Wilfred Owen's war poetry as 'passive suffering'. Rosenberg, harassed private soldier that he was, set himself to experience and to endure:

> I am determined that this war, with all its powers for devastation, shall not master my poeting – that is, if I am lucky enough to come through all right. I will not leave a corner of my consciousness covered up, but saturate myself the strange extraordinary new conditions of this life & it will all refine itself into poetry later on.' [Letter 4 to Binyon, p. 65]

He realised of course as surely as did his fellow war poets that the old pre-war traditions, including that of poetry, had been terminally undermined by the war. But where Sassoon and Owen would unleash anger and pity as weapons against what they saw as a betrayal by a Christian civilisation of its own values, Rosenberg, the Jewish outsider, took a longer, cooler look; what he called 'the dark destiny of man' (Letter N, p. 93) was not, as he knew, so easily resolved. In the trenches he had no leisure for Modernist experiment with a new poetics, as did the non-combatant American poets, Pound and Eliot. Nor did he take refuge in the straightforward relief of grief and anger. He did not lose faith in the power of his own vision, so resolutely won and held against such odds. His vocation, as he saw it, was not merely to speak for his

* *Poems* by Isaac Rosenberg, paperback (London: Chatto & Windus, 1972), p. 7.

fellow soldiers, as did Owen. It was to explore the tragedy of human existence through his acute sensuous apprehension of its vigorous beauty and mortality, captured by his painter's eye, intensified by the wartime reality of violence and its human cost:

> What fierce imaginings their dark souls lit
> Earth! Have they gone into you?
> Somewhere they must have gone . . .

In his last great poems he is shaping his language as dynamically as he shaped his drawing, to express his sense of the complexity of the experience, distilled into verse made more resonant by his compassion and control. It may serve as a fitting epitaph for the poet himself:

> None saw their spirits' shadow shake the grass,
> Or stood aside for the half used life to pass
> Out of those doomed nostrils and the doomed mouth,
> When the swift iron burning bee
> Drained the wild honey of their youth.
>
> ['Dead Man's Dump', Appendix, p. 143]

ISAAC ROSENBERG

Unpublished Material at the British Library

The first section contains letters and a draft poem to Laurence Binyon. The second section contains letters and draft poems to Gordon Bottomley. The third contains biographical material on Rosenberg assembled by Laurence Binyon, from family and friends of Rosenberg, for his Memoir in the 1922 Heinemann edition (PR22). Like the manuscripts in other collections (see p. 27) the letters and draft poems are largely written in pencil on loose leaves and scraps of paper, some torn from notebooks, some on headed notepaper Rosenberg found at the YMCA or Church Army huts behind the lines. Many are creased and stained from being folded and carried in Rosenberg's tunic pockets or pack. (Some of the typescript poem versions, which were all produced by Annie Rosenberg for her brother, may have been sent directly by her to Gordon Bottomley at Rosenberg's request.)

Both Bottomley and Binyon kept everything Rosenberg sent them for their own interest and in order to preserve them for his future use, as he had no way of keeping hold of his material in the trenches, and they did try to keep letters and drafts in chronological order, with their envelopes for the postmarks. ('It is real friendship of you to take that workable interest in my poetry & trouble to look after my things,' wrote Rosenberg to Bottomley in the summer of 1917, Letter N, p. 94.) Rosenberg's spelling and grammar were by no means as bad as his earlier editors sometimes made out; they were certainly, like his punctuation, occasionally erratic, but it is obvious from the letters that this was frequently a result of haste and the circumstances of trench life – hardly conducive to reflection and proof reading. The older writers were more troubled by Rosenberg's slips of spelling and grammar than perhaps a modern reader would be, and their letters to each other (pp. 124–6) show that they did take their editorial task most seriously.

They and his other mentors have often been accused of patronising Rosenberg, but they were publishing the work of an unknown poet in a more formal age and would have felt that leaving intact obvious grammatical and punctuation errors might prejudice the contemporary reader against him. From Rosenberg's grateful response to their criticism in this correspondence it is understandable that they should feel that the younger poet would have accepted their editorial corrections, especially for publication. Bottomley did 'correct' the poems for the 1922 edition, perhaps somewhat overdoing it, as he admitted to Harding in 1936 (quoted by Noakes, *PPIR*, p. xvi). For the 1937 edition (*CW37*), his co-editor Denys Harding returned to the original poetry texts as far as possible, as did Ian Parsons in the 1979 revised edition (*CW79*). Yet there were still many textual inconsistencies and problems with dating and order, which have been fully discussed by Dr Vivien Noakes in her comprehensive new edition of the poems and plays (*PPIR*), published in 2004.

The letters were another matter. Presumably because Binyon had mislaid this bundle of manuscripts after the completion of the 1922 edition (*PR22*), there was no opportunity for Harding and Bottomley to recheck their texts. So none of this manuscript material, published or unpublished, was available for their 1937 edition of the *Collected Works* (*CW37*). It therefore reproduces the Binyon and Bottomley letter extracts exactly as printed in the 1922 edition (*PR22*). The last editor to deal with the letters, Ian Parsons in the 1979 edition, while restoring the text of the poems, explained in his Editor's Note that his intention was to make the letters easy to understand: 'this has involved a certain (though very limited) amount of "editing" in the matter of punctuation, spelling, and the occasional grammatical solecism' (*CW79*, pp. xxxii). I believe that the vitality of Rosenberg's style comes through more completely because of his urgency and haste, and therefore with the rediscovered letters I have taken the opportunity to reproduce Rosenberg's letters as he wrote them, preferring to indicate the odd slip rather than correct it. On comparing the originals to the published extracts there are one or two minor changes which are indicated in the heading notes to each letter. Where Rosenberg has erased a word or phrase in the letters and it is still legible I have included it thus: <word> [crossed out]. Where a line or word has been crossed out by the censor I have so indicated in the text.

As Dr Noakes's edition (*PPIR*) is now authoritative, I have compared the texts of the poems and draft poems to her final versions, and included these variations in the heading notes to each poem. The final published versions are included in the Appendix below, p. 137. Although these newly discovered manuscripts were not available when Dr Noakes was preparing her edition, the fullest versions of the poems included here are in fact the same as her final versions except for some very minor variations in punctuation. Happily this is also true of the versions published in my own Enitharmon edition of the *Selected Poems and Letters* in 2003 (*SPL*). Several of the draft poems also relate to drafts in other collections, and the best guide to the complexity of all the variant holographs and typescripts in other collections is Dr Noakes, who has provided the fullest annotations on variant drafts in her edition. While there are no completely unknown poems among the rediscovered manuscripts published here, there are some unknown passages and unpublished variants, notably to 'Break of Day in the Trenches' and 'Dead Man's Dump', which are highlighted in the individual heading notes to each letter and draft poem.

All letters and poems are holograph pencil in Isaac Rosenberg's hand unless otherwise stated (IR). Each letter and draft poem is described in individual heading notes. There are also footnotes for further information. The text in normal typeface is already published in previous editions, and the text marked in bold is unpublished.

SYMBOLS

The texts of the poems are compared to the definitive versions established by Vivien Noakes in *PPIR* (abbreviations of publications, p. 8). These final versions are included in the Appendix (p. 137).

THE POEMS

l. or ll. ooo	line numbers ooo
<word>	word or words in this version altered in *PPIR*
<<word>>	word or words cancelled or amended within a phrase, the whole of which is later cancelled in *PPIR*
'word'	word as in *PPIR*
<<*word*>>	word crossed out in MS by IR in his own hand
{word}	word added by IR above or below a line
(words and lines ooo)	words and lines added or omitted in *PPIR*
'Title of Poem'	title of poem as in *PPIR*

THE LETTERS

<word or phrase>	[crossed out or erased] in IR's hand.
[sic]	indicating IR's original spelling and punctuation
[editor's comment]	in square brackets

Letters to Laurence Binyon

Six letters and one draft poem, numbered 1 to 6,
poem enclosed with letter 5.

The bundle of manuscripts stored by Laurence Binyon at the British Museum contains six letters from Rosenberg to Binyon. Three are from 1912–13, when Rosenberg first met Binyon, and discussed both his poetry and the visual arts with him. These are written in ink in a loose and vigorous hand that still bears some relation to the copperplate Rosenberg would have learnt at school. Letters 1 and 2 were sent from the Mile End address where Rosenberg lived with his family; letter 3 is sent from the studio room he rented for a while in Carlingford Road, Hampstead, from July to December 1912. The remaining two are in pencil and date from the autumn and winter of 1916 when Rosenberg was stationed in France, where he had arrived with his battalion of the King's Own Royal Lancasters in July 1916. It seems likely that Rosenberg would have continued to correspond with Binyon, whom he found sympathetic both to his writing and his art; moreover Binyon's wartime service as a Red Cross volunteer meant that he could understand, as most of Rosenberg's Home Front correspondents could not, the unique circumstances of the Western Front. Rosenberg acknowledges this in Letter 4 (p. 66):

> If I get the chance I'll write a sequence of poems of trench life which I mean to be a startler. You know all that goes on so I won't worry you with my experience now, but they the poems will be pysological [sic] & individual and I hope interesting.

No other letters survive, nor does Binyon refer to any others in his *Memoir* of 1922 (*PR22*). It's possible that Binyon's Red Cross mission to France in May 1917 interrupted their correspondence, and when

Rosenberg came home on leave in September 1917 he would be able to visit Binyon at the British Museum, so there would be no need to write. But Binyon's commitment to Rosenberg is made clear by the exchange of letters with Bottomley in 1919 and the material he gathered from family and friends of Rosenberg for the 1922 edition, here published for the first time.

Of the six letters to him, Binyon only published a paragraph of Letter 1 and just over half of Letter 4 – but the latter is one of Rosenberg's great letters, containing his indomitable statement of principle: 'I am determined that this war, with all its powers for devastation, shall not master my poeting – that is if I am lucky to come through all right' (Letter 4, p. 65).

Unpublished text marked in bold

1. **Letter to Laurence Binyon**; ink, no date but dated 1912 in *CW79*, p. 192. **Unpublished lines.**

159 Oxford Street

Mile End E

Dear Sir

I must thank you very much for your encouraging reply to my poetical efforts. **Rambles in the wake of the muse generally end in ditchwater – & I expected a good sousing for my boldness in waylaying so staunch an upholder of the Muse's honour.** As you are so kind enough to ask about myself I am sending a sort of autibiography [sic] I wrote about a year ago **which I hope you will excuse not being in type.** You will see from that, that my circumstances have not been very favourable for artistic production; but generally I am optimistic, I suppose because I am young & do not yet properly realize the difficulties. I am now attending the Slade, being sent there by some wealthy Jews who are kindly interested in me, & of course I spend most of my time drawing. I find writing interferes with drawing a good deal, and is far more exhausting.

Amongst modern artists Rossetti* appeals very much to me & also his poems. I think his 'Beata Beatrix' has as much of the divine insight as any Lippi Lippi – more I should say, because in it Rossetti has deified a human passion and not as the Italians did humanized deity. I do not know how much of early Italian art, but I consider that form of art – <u>Art</u> [sic]. For emotional fervour and lyrical ecstacy [sic], expression through passionate colour and definite design, – because instead of confining themselves to rules of architectural line, they took the infinitude of nature to build their designs from; because instead of appearing an affectation of beauty – a moment frozen into canvas – they have the grace & quality – the spontaneity of unselfconscious and childlike nature – infinity of suggestion – that is as much part & voice of the artists soul [sic] as the song to the bird.

I know little of modern poets as they are difficult to get hold of – but Francis Thomson† [sic] a little – I think he is tremendous. In fact that is the sort of poetry that appeals most to me – richly coloured without losing that mysteriousness, the hauntingness which to me is the subtle music – the soul to which the colour is flesh & raiment.

I have not yet done anything in painting or drawing which I would care to show, but when I have got anything done I wonder whether you would have time to see them if I brought or sent them. Of course I would like to do imaginative work but I have hardly attempted anything – practising portraiture mostly as I feel that is the most paying – & one must live.

I sincerely hope I have not bored you.

Yours sincerely
Isaac Rosenberg.

* Dante Gabriel Rossetti, poet and painter (1828–82).
† Francis Thompson, poet (1850–1907).

2. Letter to Binyon; ink, no date but by the change from 'Dear Sir 'to 'Dear Mr Binyon' clearly follows above Letter 1 (1912) to which it relates. **Unpublished.**

159 Oxford St
Mile End E

Dear Mr Binyon

I enclose the things you promised to look at – They are all small so even if they are worthless they will not take up much of your time. I don't know whether I have quite followed your advice about being more concrete – Im [sic] afraid my mind isn't formed that way – I believe, though, my expression is more simple. My muse is a very conventional muse, far away & dreamy, she does not seek beauty in common life.

I trust it is not impertinent to bother you about private affairs but I wonder if you could give me introductions to Editors or people who might consider my things. I have sent a few times but without success – I thought they might be considered more attentively if I had an introduction. I believe I could write Art articles – if you fall in with this idea, I could send you one I am writing, and you could judge. I would be so obliged, but if you think this is too previous, I shan't trouble any more about it.

Yours sincerely
Isaac Rosenberg.

3. Letter to Binyon; ink, no date but *c.* 1912–13. **Unpublished.**

32 Carlingford Road
Hampstead

Dear Mr Binyon

I have not been able to return your poem* sooner as I have been very busy – I hope you have not been uneasy about it. Thank you so much for the pleasure it has given me. I like some of it tremendously. The opening two stanzas especially appeal to me – & the 2nd stanza

---

* Laurence Binyon,'The Mirror' (1903–13), *Collected Poems* (London: Macmillan, 1943), p. 175.

about the moon as earth's mirror – and all the end part from 'Peace is it peace'. I like the whole poem but these especially appeal to me for the rapture they rise into. I like the restraint of it as a whole & the metre. Forgive the jerky observations but I felt I had to say something even if I could not say what I felt.

Yours sincerely

Isaac Rosenberg.

4. **Letter to Binyon**; pencil, no date but dated in CW79 Autumn 1916; probably November; published with some minor errors in CW79, p. 248. **Unpublished lines.**

22311 A Coy 3 platoon

11th Batt KORL. BEF

Dear Mr Binyon

It is far – very far to the British Museum from here – (situated as I am, Siberia is no further – & certainly not colder) but not too far for that tiny mite of myself – my letter, to reach there. Winter has found its way into the trenches at last, but I will spare you & leave to your immagination [sic], the transport of delight with which we welcomed its coming. Winter is not the least of the horrors of war.

I am determined that this war, with all its powers for devastation, shall not master my poeting – that is if I am lucky enough to come through all right. I will not leave a corner of my consciousness covered up, but saturate myself with the strange extraordinary new conditions of this life & it will all refine itself into poetry later on. I have thoughts of a play round our Jewish hero, Judas Maccabeus. <for a hero> [crossed out]. I have much real material here, & also there is some parrallel [sic] in the savagery of the invaders then to this war. I am not decided whether truth of period is a good quality or a negative one. Flaubert's 'Salambo' proves, perhaps, that it is good. It decides the tone of the work, though it makes it hard to give the human side and make it more living. However it is impossible now to work and difficult even to think of poetry, one is so cramped intellectually.

The period is about Christ's time & I think I could bring about a meeting between Christ & Judas, in fact Christ could be brought up or spend part of his boyhood with Mathias the High Priest & father of Judas.

I am enclosing a poem I think will please you, it being simpler than my usual.

I saw some time ago in the papers a book of yours had appeared. Your time in France has borne fruit which I hope to taste when I go home on leave if that time ever comes.

If I get the chance I'll write a sequence of poems of trench life which <will> [crossed out] I mean to be a startler. You know all that goes on so I won't worry you with my experiences now, but they the poems will be pysological [sic] & individual & I hope interesting. I hope you will write when you can though I suppose your time is filled up.

Yours sincerely, I Rosenberg.

5. Letter to Binyon; pencil, with envelope dated from postmark 5 December 1916 [envelope in two fragments, one bearing faint words in pencil <fat paint brush>, <pocket knife> in unknown hand]. Unpublished.
Poem enclosed 'Daughters of War': unpublished variant.

22311 3 Platoon A Coy
11th KORL BEF

Dear Mr Binyon

I have thought about the poem & your suggestions but it is impossible for me to work on it here. If you care to you could send it to a paper – I might yet get something for it, which would come in handy when I go home on leave – if I do.

We are in a rougher shop than before & the weather is about as bad as it can be but my Pegasus though it may kick at times will not stampede or lose or leave me. I felt your letter very much but we are young & its [sic] excitement for us. I have also learnt a good deal about human nature though perhaps not very flattering to it.

I wonder if you like this new poem. It has my usual fault of intricacy I know but I think the idea is clear. Mr Gibsons [sic] new book 'Battle' was sent me most of the poems are really fine and absolutely express the thing. 'Between the Lines' is most vivid & exact. I was never very fond of Gibson's work, it struck me as cultured vigour – but I was delighted with this book.*

Yours sincerely Isaac Rosenberg.

5. Poem 'Daughters of War' enclosed with Letter 5, above, 5 December 1916. [This version differs also from version IR sent to Bottomley on 5 December 1916, see p. 87.] Holograph in pencil as published in *PPIR*, pp. 42–5 except for: l. 1 <in vain> cancelled; l. 2 <in> for 'their' and <new bared> for 'naked'; (*PPIR* has 11 additional lines between ll. 3–4); l. 5 <have blown> cancelled for 'blow to'; ll. 9 & 10 <strong immortal girls/Their wrists in an easy might> cancelled for 'strong everliving Amazons/And in an easy might their wrists'; l. 12 <the wild soft lustres> for 'the wild – the soft lustres'; l. 16 <our perishing> repeated twice for 'our corroding' once; ll. 18–19 <that must be utterly perished/For the soul to rush out> for 'that must be broken – broken for evermore/For the soul to leap out'; l. 21 <though> for 'tho'; l. 22 <Kinglier than spirits crowned> for 'Best sculptures of Deity'; l. 24 <archangels> for 'Archangels'; (*PPIR* has additional 22 lines after l. 27). Unpublished variant.

Daughters of War

Space beats in vain the ruddy freedom of their limbs
In naked dances with man's spirit new bared
By the root side of the tree of life.
The old bark burnt with iron wars
They have blown to a live flame   5
To mar the young green days.
We were satisfied of our Lords the moon and the sun

---

* W. W. Gibson, *Battle*, op. cit., see p. 53.

To take our wage of sleep and bread and warmth –
These maidens came – these strong immortal girls
Their wrists in an easy might   10
Of night's sway & moon's sway the sceptres brake,
Clouding the wild soft lustres of our eyes.

Clouding the wild lustres, the clinging tender lights;
Driving the darkness into the flame of day,
With the Amazonian wind of them   15
Over our perishing faces
Over our perishing faces
That must be utterly perished
For the soul to rush out
Into their huge embraces.   20
Though there are human faces
Kinglier than spirits crowned
And sinews lusted after
By the archangels tall
Even these must leap to the love-heat of these maidens   25
From the flame of terrene days,
Leaving gray ashes to the wind . . . to the wind.

6. **Letter to Binyon;** pencil, no date, postmark, or heading, on scrap torn from notebook, but must follow above letters in sequence, probably in December 1916; [the poem that appeared in *Poetry* (Chicago) December 1916 was 'Break of Day in the Trenches']. **Unpublished.**

Dear Mr Binyon
Please don't bother about the poem if you still mean to try & get it printed. 'Poetry' of America are [sic] printing it and it might cause complaint if it were printed again.

I am feeling a bit knocked up but I hope Ill get over it.

When will this plague be over – everybody & everything seems tumbling to pieces.

Yours sincerely
Isaac Rosenberg.

Letters to Gordon Bottomley

Twenty-eight letters and seventeen drafts of poems,
marked alphabetically A to Y; poems marked as the
letters with which they are enclosed.

The sequence of twenty-eight letters to Bottomley all date from Rosenberg's army service in France; they run from July 1916, a month after he arrived, until his death near Arras in March 1918. Of these sixteen have never been published, and of the remaining eleven only one, Letter K (February 1917), has been published in its entirety. There are seventeen drafts of poems including unpublished variants.

Gordon Bottomley kept the envelopes and the usually undated letters and their draft poem enclosures together so that the latter could be dated from their postmark. (Rosenberg wrote to Sydney Schiff, another correspondent, 'I am sorry I can't date my letters as you ask but I never know the date and one can't choose your time as to sending letters', *CW79*, p. 244.) One dated letter (W, 17 February 1918, p. 117) has survived with its envelope postmarked 19 February; thus it may be assumed that the remarkable army postal service delivered letters in about two to three days, and that Rosenberg's letters were usually written some two days before the postmark. Bottomley himself also dated some letters sent to him and listed all letters with enclosures and envelopes alphabetically in his own hand, from A to Y, with occasional subsidiary numbering. The latter seems to occur when groups of letters or loose leaves clearly belong together; for example R2, R3 and R4 (pp. 106–7) all date from Rosenberg's ten days' home leave in September 1917. However this is not wholly consistent, for R1 (p. 105) does not. In *PR22*, *CW37* and *CW79* (p. 257), it is recorded as being to Edward Marsh, June 1917, but the manuscript is clearly addressed to Bottomley and postmarked 19 August 1917.

It is clear that in spite of Bottomley's care the pencil manuscripts, often rubbed and torn, in envelopes disintegrating from the damp of the trenches, were confusing. For example, Letter A relates to a fragment of envelope postmarked 12 July 1916. In PR22, CW37 and CW79 editions the postmark is mistakenly given as 12 June 1916, but the original postmark is clear, so I have amended it with a note to that effect. Bottomley has marked the envelope A & B; poem A, 'Fret the nonchalant noon', is itself written on a piece of torn envelope. Page 2 of letter A contains the poem 'The Troopship', and I have therefore presumed that both were received in the same envelope in June, and the error of July crept in to PR22. Finally, the only other major change in chronology refers to Letters F, G, H, I, N, O, P, which were mislettered non-chronologically by Bottomley. Because this is important not only for the narrative, but also for the genesis of the poems Rosenberg is enclosing and discussing, I have reordered them chronologically, but included Bottomley's lettering in brackets. Bottomley's annotations and my emendations are clearly indicated in the headings to each letter.

Poem variants indicated in the headings to each poem (or to the letter if the poem is part of the letter): comparison is with the final versions established by Dr Vivien Noakes in PPIR, which are also included in the Appendix (p. 138). All letters and poems are holograph pencil in IR's hand unless otherwise stated.

Unpublished text marked in bold

A. Letter to Bottomley with fragment of envelope marked A & B by Bottomley, postmarked 12 July 1916. **Unpublished lines.**
(CW79 extract p. 236, where dated 'postmark 12 June 1916' – but above date more likely, corresponding with envelope A postmark.)

22311 Pte I Rosenberg
c/o 40th Divisional Coy Salvage Officer
BEF France

Dear Mr Bottomley

If you really mean what you say in your letter, there is no need to tell you how proud I am. I had to read your letter many times before I could convince myself you were not 'pulling my leg'. People are always telling me my work is promising – incomprehensible, but promising, and all that sort of thing, and my meekness subsides before the patronising knowingness. The first thing I saw of yours was last year in the Georgian Book,* 'The End of the World' I must have worried all London about it – certainly everybody I knew. I had never seen anything like it. After that I got hold of 'Chambers of Imagery.'† Mr Marsh told me of your plays, but I joined the Army and have never been able to get at them. It is a great thing to me to be able to tell you now in this way what marvellous pleasure your work has given me, and what pride that my work pleases you. I had ideas for a play called 'Adam and Lilith' before I came to France, but I must wait now. I **had heard about your weakness with pain, & I beg of you not to trouble yourself to answer if it exhausts you, though a word from you gives me pride and pleasure.**

Yours sincerely Isaac Rosenberg.

A. Poem on p. 2 of letter: 'The Troopship' as published in *PPIR*, p. 127 (see Appendix p. 137) except: l. 3 no comma after 'sleep'; l. 9 no apostrophe in 'winds'.

> Here is a sketch
> 'The Troopship'
>
> Grotesque and queerly huddled
> Contortionists to twist

---

*   *Georgian Poetry 1911–12*, vol 1, op. cit., see p. 20.
†   Gordon Bottomley, *Chambers of Imagery*, see p. 93.

The sleepy soul to a sleep
We lie all sorts of ways
But cannot sleep.   5
The wet wind is so cold,
And the lurching men so careless,
That, should you drop to a doze,
Winds fumble or men's feet
Is on your face.   10

A. Poem fragment on piece of envelope; as in *PPIR*, p. 131 except: ll. 2, 3, 4 <thy> for 'your'; l.9 <will> for 'shall'; l. 10 'old' inserted before 'space' in *PPIR*; ten more verses inserted after l. 10 in *PPIR* (Appendix p. 146). **Unpublished words.**

Fret the nonchalant noon
With **thy** spleen
Or **thy** gay brow
For the motion of **thy** spirit
Ever moves with these   5

When day shall be too quiet –
Deaf to you
And your dumb smile
Untuned air **will** lap the stillness
In the space for your voice   10

B. Letter to Bottomley dated from postmark in Bottomley's hand 'Field Post Office 23 July 1916 Passed Field Censor 3858'; on headed notepaper: Church Army and CEMS Recreation Hut. 'Ive' without apostrophe in MS, *CW79*, p. 238. **Unpublished paragraphs.**

22311 Pte I Rosenberg
c/o 40th Divisional Coy Salvage Officer
BEF
[word erased by censor]

Dear Mr Bottomley

Your letter came to-day with Mr Trevelyan's, like two friends to take me for a picnic. Or rather like friends come to release the convict from his chains with his innocence in their hands, as one sees in the twopenny picture palace. You might say, friends come to take you to church, or the priest to the prisoner. Simple *poetry* – that is where an interesting complexity of thought is kept in tone and right value to the dominating idea so that it is understandable and still ungraspable. I know it is beyond my reach just now, except, perhaps, in bits. I am always afraid of being empty. When I get more leisure in more settled times I will work on a larger scale and give myself **more** room then I may be less frustrated in my efforts to be clear, and satisfy myself too. I think what you say about getting beauty by phrasing of passages rather than the placing of individual words very fine and very true.

The poem 'In the Trenches', I altered a little and have asked my sister to send on to you. I left a line out 'a shell's haphazard fury' after 'Irrevocable earth buffet'. I don't think I made my meaning quite clear that it is a shell bursting which has only covered my [sic] & the poppy I plucked at the beginning of poem still in my ear with dust. It is one of a sequence of dramatic war poems I want to write. 'Marching' 'the Troopship', 'Fret the nonchalant noon'. [sic] In the Trenches are written. I have plenty of ammusing [sic] & serious material. Last night we had a funny hunt for fleas. All stripped by candlelight some Scots dancing over the candle & burning the fleas, & the funniest, drollest and dirtiest scenes of conversation ever immagined [sic]. Burns 'Jolly Beggars' is nothing to it. I have heaps of material. I feel all your advice and am very grateful for it. If you knew how much I have destroyed because I felt it would be completely unintelligable [sic] to most, you would anyway praise my prudence. I have not read 'King Lear's Wife' & I have never seen the second Georgian book. Since Ive joined the only book I carried with me & read was your 'Chambers of Imagery' with the Nimrod poem. I lost it when I came to France. For the last week or two Ive been in a quieter but more interesting job than trenches. Ive got to rummage behind the lines among shattered houses & ruins for salvage. We come across all kinds of grim & funny odds & ends. <We go> [crossed out] More material for poem. I don't know how long this job will last but its fairly safe anyway. [sic] except for Stray shells which don't count. I do trust you are not worried by ill health and are happy.

Yours sincerely
Isaac Rosenberg.

B (mislettered A by Bottomley). Poem enclosed 'In the Trenches'; a variant of 'Break of Day in the Trenches' in *PPIR*, p. 128 (Appendix p. 137); l. 4 {uncanny} written below 'sardonic' in MS; otherwise as in *PPIR* except for: l. 7 <Droll subterranean> cancelled; ll. 8, 9 <*Queer rat, they*> for 'Droll rat, they'; l. 11 <(and Lord knows what antipathies)> cancelled; l. 12 <For> cancelled for 'Now'; l. 13 <And> cancelled for 'You'; l. 15 <the poppy bloodied field> cancelled for 'sleeping green'; l. 16 <Our hands will touch through your feet> cancelled; l. 20 <Helpless whims> cancelled for 'Bonds to the'; ll. 24–28 amended in final version. **Unpublished variant.**

In the Trenches

The darkness crumbles away,
It is the same old Druid time as ever,
Only a live thing leaps my hand,
A queer sardonic rat
    {uncanny}
As I pull a poppy from the parapet   5
To stick behind my ear:
Droll subterranean;
<<*Queer rat, they*>>

They would shoot you if they knew
Your cosmopolitan sympathies   10
(And Lord knows what antipathies)
For you have touched an English hand,
And will do the same to a German
Soon, no doubt, if it be your pleasure
To cross the poppy blooded field between,   15
Our hands will touch through your feet,
It seems, odd thing, you grin as you pass
Strong eyes, fine limbs, haughty athletes
Less chanced than you for life,
Helpless whims of murder   20
Sprawled in the bowels of the earth
The torn fields of France.
What do you see in our eyes
At the hiss, the irrevocable swiftness,
<<As>>
The laconic earth buffet.   25
A shell!
Safe. Again murder has overlooked us
Only white with powder & chalk.

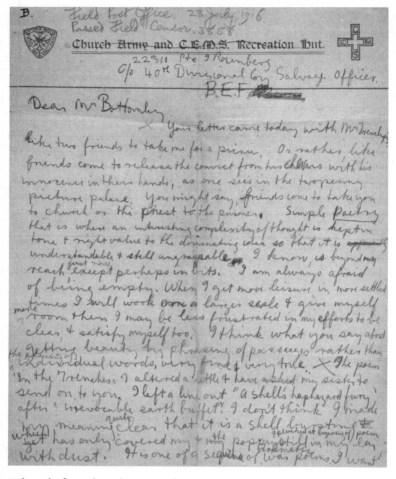

Holograph of Rosenberg's letter to Gordon Bottomley, Letter B, postmarked '23 July 1916'. Credit: British Library.

to write. 'Marching' 'The troop Ship.' 'Fret the nonchalant'
& 'In the Trenches' are written. I have plenty of amusing
& serious material. Last night we had a funny hunt
for fleas. All stripped by candlelight some dancing over
the candle, & the funniest, drollest & smallest songs &
conversation ever immagined. Burns 'Jolly Beggars'
is nothing to it. I have heaps of material.
I feel all your advice & am very grateful for it. If you
knew how much I have destroyed because I felt
it would be wholly completly unintelligable to most,
you would anyway — praise my prudence
I have not read 'Kingsters wife' & have never seen
the Second Georgian book. Since I've joined the only
book I carried with me & read, was your 'Chamber
of Imagery' with the Nimrod poem. I lost it
when I came to France. For the last week or two
I've been on a quieter but more interesting job than
trenches. I've got to rummage behind the lines
amongst shattered houses & ruins for salvage.
We come across all kinds of grim & funny odds
& ends. Fine material for poem. I don't know how
long this job will last but its fairly safe, anyway
except for strong shells which don't count. I do trust
you are not worried by ill health & are happy
Yours sincerely Isaac Rosenberg

In the Trenches

The darkness crumbles away,
It is the same old Druid Time as ever,
Only a live thing leaps my hand,
A queer ~~sardonic~~ rat
As I pull a poppy from the parapet
To stick behind my ear,
~~Droll subterranean~~

They would shoot you if they knew
Your cosmopolitan sympathies
(And Lord knows what antipathies)
For you have touched an English hand,
And will do the same to a German
Soon, no doubt, if it be your pleasure
To cross the poppy blooded field between,
Our hands will touch through your feet,
It seems odd thing, you grin, as you pass
Strong eyes, fine limbs, haughty athletes
Less chanced than you for life,
Helpless whims of Murder,
Sprawled in the bowels of the earth

p.t.o.

Holograph in pencil of poem 'In the Trenches', Poem B, enclosed with Letter B (see p. 74).
Credit: British Library.

The torn fields of France.
What do you see in our eyes
At the hiss, the irrevocable swiftness,
As the laconic earth buffet,
As still
Safe. Again murder has overlooked us
Only white with powder & chalk

C. Letter to Bottomley dated in Bottomley's hand 'France Aug 8 1916'; envelope postmarked 8 August 1916; on headed notepaper: Church Army and CEMS Recreation Fund. **Unpublished.**

Dear Mr Bottomley

Since writing to you the new Georgian book arrived.* 'King Lear's Wife' is a fine criticism of the Elizabethan manner of writing. You don't waste a word of it is equal throughout. [sic] The conception of Lear making love beside the dying Queen's bedside is terrific. The tone of cruelty throughout the play, the marvelous [sic] portraiture of Goneril, the vividness of it all gave me a pleasure I have not experienced since I read our great masters.

You must forgive me if you can my sisters pestering letter about printing and selling my work. She told me what you said & the whole affair has vexed me very much. I simply <told> [crossed out] asked her to send a clean copy of my poem to you, as I scrawl abominably, and I suppose she has some sort of notion that one can't be a poet unless things are printed in daily papers. I am very sorry indeed that you have been bothered in this silly way.

I hope when I come back to England I will be allowed to make a drawing of you; as a rule the poets are unlucky in their painters; but I am eager to draw the poets I like.

Yours sincerely
Isaac Rosenberg.

D. Letter to Bottomley with envelope postmarked 15 August 1916. **Unpublished.**

Dear Mr Bottomley

I wish I were in London now and had plenty of time to put my thoughts about your book in shape. I have not had time to read it again since I last wrote to you but I am very glad you did send it as

---

* *Georgian Poetry 1913–15*, vol. 2, op. cit., see p. 20.

it is, and am very grateful and honoured. A friend sent me the Georgian book a few weeks ago, but it is so awkward out here to have books in cloth that I must send it back again. In fact at any time I prefer cheap bound books I can spoil by reading anywhere. I often find bibles in dead mens clothes [sic] & I tear the parts out I want and carry them about with me. I am pretty fagged just now, having just got back from a wild goose chase up the trenches after some stuff. Yesterday we had a lively time carrying chaps to the hospital in a handcart; its [sic] a toss up whether you're going to be the carried or the carrier. I wish you would try your hand at that Flea hunt. I don't think Ill [sic] write anything till we've settled down again. It is a thing Goya would go mad on.

I forgot to say I had not read Wells' Biblical play,* except the bits in Swinburne's essay on him. A friend sent me Swinburne out here &. Whitman. I could not help comparing Faustine with a thing I read of yours about those small Tanagra Greek figures in Chambers of Imagery. Yours gives the idea in a much more perfect manner. Swinburne writes too much for the ladies.+ I shan't try your eyes or your patience with more than this.

Yours sincerely
Isaac Rosenberg.

+<makes? so much of the sentiment tawdry. I think . . . But Swinburne is gorgeous> [erased and overwritten].

E. **Letter to Bottomley** dated from postmark 29 August 1916; no heading or address; second sheet on headed notepaper: Church Army and CEMS Recreational Hut.

---

* Charles Wells, *Joseph and his Brethren*, 1824 (republished World's Classics, Oxford University Press 1908, with an introduction by A. C. Swinburne). Wells was a friend of Keats, and this his only published verse, which was rediscovered by D. G. Rossetti and acclaimed in Swinburne's introduction as 'a great dramatic poem . . .[recalling] the more equable cadences of Shakespeare at his earliest period' (p. ix).

E. Poem 'Pozières' holograph on first page of letter; as published in *PPIR* p. 133 (Appendix p. 138) except: l. 2 '!' substituted for comma after 'women'; l. 3 < marvelous > for 'marvellous'.
Unpublished paragraphs .

Pozières

Glory! glory! glory!
British **women,** in your wombs you plotted
This monstrous girth of glory, this **marvelous** glory,
Not for mere love-delights Time meant the profound hour
When an Englishman was planned.   5
Time shouted it to his extremest outpost.
The illuminated call through the voided years
Was heard, is heard at last,
And will be heard at the last
Reverberated through the Eternities,   10
Earth's immortality and Heaven's.

Dear Mr Bottomley

Our armies deserve something better than I can hymn them;* still here is my little mite. I wrote it immediately I had sent my last letter off to you, and now I have just got your new and kind letter I take this chance of letting you see it and thanking you at the same time for your letter. By now you will have received my letter acknowledging your book, which I would rather have as it is than the < chunky > [crossed out] awkward Georgian form. < what you wish for a theatre > [crossed out] If we had a theatre as you suggest I believe we would get the great age of poetry back again. I thought Yeats had started something of the kind – the theatre I mean, not the great age.

I have read Abercrombies [sic] comedy. He writes like Hercules rolling down Hampstead hill. I doubt whether the slang always suits the grandeur and vehemence of his writing. But I always enjoy (especialy [sic] out here) his work; & the wit in this play is

* The Battle of Pozières Ridge on the Somme, 23 July – 3 September 1916.

82

strong and robust. It is a rare & enchanting work. We are still salving France & our peregrinations find us in the trenches about twice a week; we hope it won't be long before will [sic] be salving the German Trenches.

My address is still

c/o 40th divisional coy officer B.E.F.

pte I Rosenberg 22311

Please don't trouble to write unless it ammuses [sic] you to, although the arrival of a letter from you is a real deep pleasure. If I get the chance I will draw a sketch of anything I think might interest you. I leave the Flea hunt for home coming if that event ever comes about. I have a little drawing at home I should like you to accept & when next I write home I will ask them to send it to you if it can be found. It is a drawing of <the >[crossed out] Adam & Eve* when first they see each other & rush in frenzy to meet. If it cannot be found I will find it on my return as I am sure you would like it.

Yours sincerely

Isaac Rosenberg.

F. **Letter card to Bottomley** (mislettered H by Bottomley); Field Service Post Card dated 16 and 18 September 1916. Acknowledging safe receipt of parcel. **Unpublished.**

G. **Letter to Bottomley** with envelope, dated from postmark 17 and 20 September 1916. 'Ive' without apostrophe in MS. **Unpublished.**

22311 A Coy 3 Platoon

11th KORL BEF

Dear Mr Bottomley

I have not had the chance till now of thanking you for your beautiful thought of me in your letter & book. It has been wet and mucky in the trenches for some time & the cold weather helping, we are

---

* Drawing now in the Prints and Drawings Department, British Museum.

teased by the elements as well as by the German fireworks, I don't think Ive [sic] been dry yet these last few days. I have been able in heavy lidded spasms to dip half asleep into Joseph. It is magnificent; the barbarous blazonry of Marlowe too much perhaps. I came across Swinburne's notice in an old 'Fortnightly'. There is a fine freshness and vehemence in the wording of Joseph & I am looking forward to reading it properly. I did mean to write Poziers [sic] as a hymn with <good> [crossed out] ample proportions, but got stuck somehow. It gave me fine pleasure that you liked my drawing. I have not yet written home about that Adam & Eve drawing as I don't remember where it is but I want you to have it when I get back if I am lucky. I must draw the 'Flea Hunt' if I don't write it, but so far Ive [sic] not been able to do anything interesting. I forgot about your fine louse song, which naturally the world would read with visions of * Keatings floating in its mind.

I am most eager to read your early book but it would be far from safe to send it here, beside the little time there is for reading.

Yours sincerely
Isaac Rosenberg.

H. **Letter to Bottomley** (mislettered F by Bottomley) dated from postmark 12 November 1916.

H. **Poem** (mislettered F by Bottomley); '**The Destruction of the Babylonian Hordes**' included in letter as published in *PPIR* p. 137, (Appendix p. 139) except for: ll. 4 & 7 <<*words*>> crossed out by IR in MS; l. 13 'bright-heavened'; ll. 20–21 <While Solomons towers were swung between / To a gird . . . > cancelled for 'While Solomon's towers crashed between / The gird . . .' **Unpublished.**

---

* Word illegible

3 platoon
22311 A coy 11 KORL
BEF

Dear Mr Bottomley

I have a few minutes now for a wonder, to do what I like with, and I'm <spending> [crossed out] going to worry you in them with my staggering calligraphy. I asked my people at home to forward my 'Adam and Eve' done some months ago. Whether they have done so I have not heard. I heard from Mr Marsh that he had heard from you and I was mightily pleased to hear anything about you. Of course, being the Prime Minister's secretary he is far too busy to write much.* <I am sharing you!> [crossed out] We are getting well into November now and have already had it bitter cold in the trenches & warm again & wet. We are now on a long march & have done a good deal towards flattening the roads of France. I wrote a little thing yesterday which still needs working on.

The Destruction of Jerusalem by the Babylonian hordes

They left their Babylon bare
Of all its tall men.
Of all its proud horses;
They made for <<*Babylon*>> Lebanon.

And shadowy sowers went   5
Before their spears to sow
<<*Fruit that turns the lips to ash*>>
The fruit whose taste is ash
For Judah's soul to know.

They who bowed to the Bull god,   10
Whose wings roofed Babylon
In endless hosts darkened
The bright heavened Lebanon.

---

* Edward Marsh had in fact been transferred to the Colonial Office in late 1916 when Asquith's government fell.

They washed their grime in pools
Where laughing girls forgot   15
The wiles they used for Solomon.
Sweet laughter! remembered not.

Sweet laughter charred in the flame
That clutched the cloud & earth
While Solomon's towers were swung between   20
To a gird of Babylon's mirth.

I have also written or rather sketched a thing I fancy will be strong but I'll reserve that for another letter. I do hope you can fight the winter well. I hate the cold.

I have not yet been able to read the 'Joseph' thing. Our time is absolutely filled up and there is little room for Pegasus to ride in or to watch him riding. But I see now why you asked me when you read 'Moses'. <because> [crossed out] There is certainly a semblance of aim, if I may say so, I mean the matter & the subject are not so unalike and yet unusual. I hope you are writing & that I may some-day have the delight of seeing it.

Yours sincerely
Isaac Rosenberg.

I. **Letter to Bottomley** dated 5 December 1916 (with envelope post-marked 8 December 1916). **Unpublished.**

Dear Mr Bottomley

I know what it costs you to write a letter especially now this cruel weather has set in. Mr Trevelyan gave me good & cheering news of you, and also all the literary adventures at The Sheiling. Since I last wrote to you I have been feeling pretty crotchety – & my memory has become very weak and confused. I fancy the winter has bowled me over but I suppose we must go lingering on. What you say of my poem might lend colour to Marsh's belief that you are too indulgent to me, but give me half a chance and you will see it'll be the other way about. I am enclosing the poem I spoke about. I think it has nine parts of my old fault to one of my new merit; but I fancy you will like the idea.

I am grieved at the misunderstanding about Wells. I forget quite what I said but I know it was one of the rarest pieces of pleasure I have had out here, when you sent me his book.

I also received Gibson's 'Battle',* & in one way I think it the best thing the war has turned out. Personally, I think the only value in any war is the literature it results in.
'Where are all your warring kings a tale
By some stammering schoolboy told'.
[Last lines crossed out by censor and illegible.]

I. Poem 'Daughters of War' enclosed with above 5 December 1916; as published in *PPIR* p. 142 (Appendix p. 140) except for: l. 1 <in vain> cancelled; l. 2<new bared> for 'naked'; (*PPIR* has 11 additional lines between l. 3–4); l. 5 <have blown> cancelled for 'blow to' (*PPIR* has 2 additional lines between l. 6–7); l. 9 <ever-loving girls> cancelled for 'everliving Amazons'; l. 20 <though> cancelled for 'tho'; l. 21 <Kinglier than crowned spirits> cancelled for 'Best sculptures of Deity'; l. 24 <archangels> for 'Archangels'; (*PPIR* has additional 20 lines after l. 26). Unpublished variant.

Daughters of War

Space beats in vain the ruddy freedom of their limbs
In naked dances with mans spirit new bared
By the root side of the tree of life.
The old bark burnt with iron wars
They have blown to a live flame   5
To char the young green days.
We were satisfied of our Lords the moon and the sun
To take our wage of sleep & bread & warmth

---

* W. W. Gibson, *Battle*, op. cit., see p. 53.

These maidens came, these strong ever-loving girls
And in an easy might, their wrists   10
Of nights sway and moons sway the sceptres brake
Clouding the wild, the soft lustres of their eyes
Clouding the wild lustres, the clinging tender lights,
Driving the darkness into the flame of day,
With the Amazonian wind of them   15
Over our corroding faces
That must be broken – broken for evermore
So the soul can leap out
Into their huge embraces.
Though there are human faces   20
Kinglier than crowned spirits,
And sinews lusted after
By the archangels tall
Even these must leap to the love heat of these maidens
From the flames of terrene days   25
Leaving grey ashes to the wind – to the wind.

J. Letter to Bottomley with envelope dated from postmark 5 January
1917.
'Ive' without apostrophe in MS. **Unpublished.**

Dear Mr Bottomley
Your letter came to me from home on New Years day [sic], and it
was the best pleasure the new year brought. I feel better than when
I last wrote to you, I fancy it was a touch of the flue [sic] I had,
but that is all over now, though I am not altogether well; and when
I get the chance of a rest I will use it well. My poem came when I
was brooding over Judas Macabeus [sic], <about whom> [crossed
out] it is all that did come of it. If I get back all right, Judas will
come too, & all I have learnt out here will be crammed into it. Ive
also thought about the louse hunt but so far Ive had no chance of
working on it properly. It could be worked into Judas & make an

entire scene. Where we are now gives us very little chance for this & also, Ive been transfered [sic] to a labour batt.

My new address now is
Pte IR 22311 7 Platoon F. Coy
40th Division Works Batt. BEF

It is a sort of navvy Batt to repair the roads. When I went bad we were just going into the trenches & I was shipped into this. Naturally we are in less danger than before, but we are practically always under fire of some sort.

Thank you for asking about books. I shan't say I don't get the time to read, but when we've done our days [sic] work & get under the tent; (we are in tents just now) it is dark and lights are not easy to get out here. In fact it is desolation every where, in diabolical state <If> [crossed out] Don't trouble to send the book, though there is nothing I'd like more. If we are ever shifted to more convenient quarters I'll remind you of your promise you may be sure. I cannot remember whose translation Ive [sic] read; but what I've read have been very few of the Greeks; I have read some of the great <plays> [crossed out] dramas, but have always felt (except in Shelley's) [sic] the translator use his English in a foreign unnatural empty way, not like the Bible translators.

I wonder if Aeschylus as a private in the army was bothered as I am by lice. I am very grateful for your good wishes and your wifes [sic].

Yours sincerely
Isaac Rosenberg.

K. Letter to Bottomley (with envelope postmarked 19th Feb, year illegible) dated in Bottomley's hand February 1917; published in CW79, pp. 252–3.

Dear Mr Bottomley
Your letters always give me a strange and large pleasure; and I shall never think I have written poetry in vain, since it has brought your

friendliness in my way. Now, feeling as I am, castaway and used up, you don't know what a letter like yours is to me. Ever since Nov, [sic] when we first started on our long marches, I have felt weak; but it seems to be some inscrutable mysterious quality of weakness that defies all doctors. I have been examined most thoroughly several times by our doctor, & there seems to be nothing at all wrong with my lungs. I believe I have strained my abdomen in some way, & I shall know of it later on. We have had desperate weather, but the poor fellows in the trenches where there are no dugouts are the chaps to pity. I am sending a very slight sketch of a louse-hunt. It may be a bit vague, as I could not work it out here, but if you can keep it till I get back I can work on it then. I do believe I could make a fine thing of Judas. Judas as a character is more magnanimous than Moses, and I believe I could make it very intense and write a lot from material out here.

Thanks very much for your <willing interest in my> [crossed out] joining in with me to rout the pest out, but I have tried all kinds of stuff; if you can think of any preparation you believe effective I'd be most grateful for it.

Yours sincerely
Isaac Rosenberg.

L. Letter to Bottomley with envelope dated from postmark 8 April 1917; part published in *CW79*, p. 253. **Unpublished paragraphs.**

Dear Mr Bottomley
I do wish I could see Mr Trevelyans [sic] **Annual; In** [sic] his last letter to me he spoke of your things and made me most eager to see them. But the bulkiness of the book, of course, makes it out of the question, my seeing it out here, beside the bad chance I have of reading it properly. Sturge Moore is a poet I like very much though I only know his 'Sycillian idyll' [sic] in GB.* I want to see Mr Trevelyan's play very much too, as I have seen very little of

* T. Sturge Moore, 'A Sicilian Idyll', *Georgian Poetry 1911–12*, vol. 1, op. cit., see p. 20.

his work. We all want this rotton [sic] business over that keeps us away from all these good things; & the lively happenings of late sound very promising.

All through this winter I have felt most crotchety, all kinds of small things kept interfering with my fitness. My hands would get chilblains or bad boots would make my feet sore; and this aggravating a general rundown-ness [sic], I have not felt too happy. <The fact> [crossed out] I have gone less warmly clad during the winter than through the summer, because of the increased liveliness on my clothes. I've <thought> [crossed out] been stung to what we call 'dumping' a great part of my clothing, as I thought it wisest to go cold than lousy. <I believe it was this> [crossed out] It may have been this that caused all the crotchetiness.

However, we've been in no danger, that is, from shell-fire, for a good long while, though so very close to most terrible fighting. But as far as houses or sign of ordinary human living <comfort> [crossed out] is concerned, we might as well be in the Sahara Desert. I think I could give some blood-curdling touches if I wishes to tell all I see, of dead buried men blown out of their graves, and more, but I will spare you all this.

I thought you would like the flea hunt, and your way of <remarking> [crossed out] commenting on it is infinitely more superior to my sketch.

I do hope when all this is over I shall be able to see you & perhaps get a drawing done of you,

Yours sincerely
Isaac Rosenberg.

M. Letter to Bottomley dated from postmark 31 May 1917.
Unpublished.

My dear Mr Bottomley
Your last letter was a real precious letter – it touched me in the way a beautiful sad relic might, say a Greek fragment. Because I am always pained to think how dependant [sic] your ease of body and

mind is upon the weather; & to hear anything <of> [crossed out] distressful happening to you and then your wonderful poem. We have learnt out here to be a bit callous & <to gr> [crossed out] have worn the edge off our teeth with much grinding, but the 'spring of tears' remains. 'Sinai' is fine & though I'd like to think my Moses is as fine as you say; I wish I could have got some of the simple greatness Sinai has. It is the first *poem* I have seen since I left England.

> 'They watched one mount the mist
> With steps like threats'*

<that is> [crossed out] Only the very greatest poets, Job, or Marlow, could have conceived an image like that. Ive [sic] had some poems sent me lately in the Poetry Review but I think the writers should be hung, or the Editor rather. They may be good soldiers but theyre [sic] poor poets. I came across some poems once in England by 'the author of 'Erebus'.† There was no name and some of the poems were after my own heart. Do you know who he is.

I am now with the Royal Engineers & we go wiring up the line at night. We took a village & the R.Es did all the wiring & some digging in front of it. I wrote a poem about some dead Germans lying in a sunken road where we dumped our wire. I have asked my sister to send it on to you, though I think it commonplace; also 'Daughters of War' which I've improved. Ive [sic] made it into a little book for you, as I like the poem. We go out at night & sleep in the day in these woods, behind the line. It is that I've had a little more time in the day to myself & am with a small loading party by ourselves that I've been able to write these two things lately. Don't worry about the insect powder. Just when they begin to get unbearable we generally get a change, & I don't think anything else is much use. My address is

Pte IR 22311

7 Platoon, 11th KORL

c/o 229 Field Coy Royal Engineers BEF

---

* Gordon Bottomley, 'Sinai', *Chambers of Imagery* , op. cit., see p. 93.
† Evangeline Ryves, *Erebus A Book of Verse,* published anonymously 1903 (republished, London: Elkin Mathews, 1913).

I suppose I must wait for home to see the Annual & your things

Yours sincerely

Isaac Rosenberg.

N. Letter to Bottomley [mislettered O by Bottomley] with envelope postmark illegible, July 1917; part published in *CW*79, p. 258. Unpublished paragraphs.

My dear Mr Bottomley

I really do not want you to write if there is any difficulty at all in writing; as I will allways [sic] believe even when no letter arrives; [sic] in your friendliness to me. Though there is little gives me more pleasure than a letter from you yet that pleasure would be marred if I thought it was at the expense of your ease. But your last letter shows you to be in good condition & happy, & I am greatly pleased at this. Above all your tremendous 'Atlantis' & the others. 'Atlantis' is in Rossetti's way of putting it, a stunner. I think it is as fine as anything you have done, and it fairly knocked me over. It is a marvellously symbolic poem of human life; or rather the dark destiny of man – it is a sad beautiful poem.*

The other poems I have not yet read, but I will follow on with letters and shall send the bits of – or rather the bit of – a play I've written. Just now it is interfered with by a punishment I am undergoing for the offence of being endowed with a poor memory, which continually causes me trouble and often punishment. I forgot to wear my gas-helmet one day; in fact, I've often forgotten it, but I was noticed one day, and seven days' pack drill is the consequence, which I do between the hours of going up the line and sleep. My memory, allways [sic] weak, has become worse since Ive [sic] been out here.

---

* Gordon Bottomley, 'Sinai' p. 30, 'Atlantis' p. 2, 'Babel' p. 26, 'Homunculus in Penumbra' p. 55, 'Babylonian Lyric' (Nimrod) p. 29, 'Avelinglas' p. 94, 'Within your Roman House' (To Edward Thomas, with a Play) p. 37, *Chambers of Imagery*, two volumes (London: Elkin Mathews, 1907 and 1912), reprinted in *Poems of Thirty Years* (London: Constable & Co., 1925).

Your poem beginning 'Within your Roman House' is a gorgeous little affair, with a most curious music 'Homunculus in Penumbra' is strange in your old extraordinary way – the naturalness of your immagination [sic] will always be a kind of whip to me, & if I ever do anything big, it will be because of your lesson.

It is real friendship of you to take that workable interest in my poetry & trouble to look after my things. I shall send you stuff when I get the chance though just now – my torturer has this moment come for me

Yours sincerely
Isaac Rosenberg.

O. Letter to Bottomley (mislettered P by Bottomley) clearly follows on from above letter N, with envelope dated from postmark 11 July 1917. **Unpublished.**

My dear Mr Bottomley

I wrote you a day or so ago but my letter was interrupted, so I follow on with this. I want you to know the deep & real pleasure your poems* gave me & I owe you much for this, because a rare pleasure like this is something indeed to me, here. I read the 'sermon on the mount' for the first time lately, & got this rare pleasure. It is indeed heroic & great philosophy. I wrote you of your 'Atlantis' which is one of the great poems in our language: Homunculus is perhaps marvellous too, certainly no poet has conceived a more difficult idea & worked it out more real, more piercingly

The other poems I enjoyed in their different ways 'All souls' is lovely; though it seems fantastic (if I may say so) to the reality of 'Homunculus'; perhaps fantastic is not the word; fanciful, perhaps 'Avenglass' is a delightful picture poem: they all gave me that enjoyment that only solid true poetry can give. I don't suppose my poems will ever be <u>poetry</u> right and proper until I shall be able to settle

---

* Bottomley, *Chambers of Imagery*, op. cit., see p. 93.

down & whip myself into more expression. As it is, my not being able to get poetry out of my head & heart causes me <continual> [crossed out] sufficient trouble out here. Not that it interferes with the actual practical work; but with forms and things I continually forget, & authority looks at [sic] from a different angle and perspective. This even may (or may not) interfere with my chances of an early leave (the earliest was late enough) but will never break the ardour of my poetry. I have not read the 'Chronicles of Jeremiah' & thank you for putting me on it. We Jews are all taught Hebrew in our childhood but I was a young rebel and would not be taught, unluckily now. I read Hebrew like a parrot without knowing the meaning. I meant to go on with Moses because I have made ambition to be the dominant point in his character, which Ive [sic] considered is very unfriendly to my ancestor. I did mean to contrast him with a christ like man, which I may yet do. However I've written a little scribble about him, and my sketch for a play is really too crude & undeveloped, & I am not sure whether I will send it. But I am expecting it any time in its typed form from home & by that time, if army rigour has not shattered all my dreams of Parnassian peregrinations, I may have thought of improvements. Perhaps you know my little poem 'Wedded' well it is a commentary on that. But the woman is not subtle enough & the man is hardly yet suggested, & the third character is a sort of castrated neuter gender, so I hardly think I will be doing good return for the marvellous 'Atlantis' & the rest.

So Abercrombie is a shell inspector; that sounds more exciting than school inspector; yet Matthew Arnold had an exciting enough time I should think. I swear he (LA) is laying up stores for great plays, gathered from his shell factories, and it gives me great happiness to think of you two together & to learn you are well.

Yours sincerely

Isaac Rosenberg.

O. **Poem: holograph poem pencil fragment** (mislettered P by Bottomley) enclosed with letter O (mislettered P by Bottomley) as *PPIR* (see Appendix p. 139) except for: l. 5 <bronze skinned and> for 'bronze, the'; l. 7 <that> for 'the'; l. 8 <<*then*>> crossed out for <<yet>> by IR ['Then' in *PPIR*].

The Jew

Moses, from whose loins I sprung
Lit by a lamp in his blood
Ten immutable rules, a moon
For mutable lampless men.

The blonde, **bronze skinned &** ruddy   5
With the same heaving blood
Keep tide to **that** moon of Moses
Yet why do they sneer at me?

P. **Letter to Bottomley** with envelope (mislettered N by Bottomley), dated from postmark 23 July 1917. Part published in *CW 79*, p. 257 (where misdated from postmark 20 July 1917). **Unpublished paragraphs.**

My dear Mr Bottomley

My sister wrote me of your note, and it made me very glad to feel you thought in that way about my poem, because I like it myself above anything I have yet done. I know my letters are not what they should be; but I must take any chance I get of writing for fear another chance does not come, so I write hastily and leave out most I should write about. I wished to say last time a lot about your poem, but I could think of nothing that would properly express my great pleasure in it; and I can think of nothing now. If anything I think it is too brief – although it is so rare and compressed and full of hinted matter. I wish I could get back and read your plays; and if my luck still continues, I shall. Leaves have commenced with us, but it may be a good while before I get mine. We are more busy now than when I last wrote, but I generally manage to knock something up if my brain means to, & I am sketching out a little play [*The Unicorn*]. My great fear is that I may lose what I've written, which can happen here so easily. I send home any bit I write, for safety, but that can easily get lost in transmission. However, I live in an immense trust that things will turn out well.

I do hope this weather suits your health & that you are not caused much trouble. Just now I have toothache but otherwise I was never so well.

Do not write because you think you ought to answer, but write when you have nothing else to do & you wish to kill time, it is no trouble to me to write these empty letters, when I have a minute to spare, just to let you know that life & poetry are as fresh as ever in me.

Yours sincerely
Isaac Rosenberg.

P. Typescript of 'Daughters of War' (mislettered N by Bottomley) enclosed with letter P above (mislettered N by Bottomley), dated in Annie Rosenberg's hand May 1917.

'Daughters of War' typescript with corrections in ink (possibly by Bottomley). As *PPIR* (see Appendix p. 140) except for: l. 1 <in vain> cancelled, 'beats' added in MS ink; l. 2 <new bared> cancelled for 'naked'; (*PPIR* has 11 additional lines between ll. 3–4); l. 5 <have blown> cancelled for 'blow to'; (*PPIR* has 2 additional lines between ll. 6–7); l. 30 < Transfiguring lit> cancelled for 'Moved and merged, gloomed and lit'; l. 31 <ppeaking> cancelled for 'speaking' corrected MS ink; (*PPIR* has one additional line between ll. 34–5); l. 38 <stick> cancelled for 'gleam'; l. 41 <ahere> for 'have' corrected in ink MS.

Daughters of War

Space beats **in vain** the ruddy freedom of their limbs
In naked dances with man's spirit **new bared**
By the root side of the tree of life.
The old bark burnt with iron wars

They **have blown** to a live flame   5
To char the young green days
We were satisfied of our Lords the moon and the sun
To take our wage of sleep and bread and warmth –
These maidens came – these strong everliving Amazons,
And in an easy might their wrists   10
Of night's sway and noon's sway the sceptres brake,
Clouding the wild – the soft lustres of our eyes.

Clouding the wild lustres, the clinging tender lights;
Driving the darkness into the flame of day,
With the Amazonian wind of them   15
Over our corroding faces
That must be broken . . . broken for evermore
So that the soul can leap out
Into their huge embraces.
Tho' there are human faces   20
Best sculptures of Deity,
And sinews lusted after
By the Archangels tall
Even these must leap to the love heat of these maidens
From the flame of terrene days,   25
Leaving gray ashes to the wind . . . to the wind.

One whose great lifted face
Where wisdom's strength and beauty's strength
And the thewed strength of large beasts
Transfiguring lit,   30
Was **ppeaking,** surely, as the earth men's earth fell away
Whose new hearing drunk the sound
Where pictures lutes and mountains mixed
With the loosed spirit of a thought.

'My sisters force their males   35
From the doomed earth, from the doomed glee

And hankering of hearts.
Frail hands **stick** up through the human quagmire and lips of ash
Seem to wail, as in sad and faded paintings
Far sunken and strange.   40
My sisters **ahere** their males
Clean of the dust of the old days
That clings about those white hands,
And yearns in those voices sad
But these shall not see them,   45
Or think of them in any days or years,
They are my sister's lovers in other days and years'

I Rosenberg (Pte)   May 1917 [in Annie Rosenberg's hand]
BEF France.

P. Typescript of 'Dead Man's Dump' (mislettered N by Bottomley) on
pink paper enclosed with letter P (mislettered N by Bottomley) above.
Corrections in ink by IR.
Typescript as printed in *PPIR*, p. 139 (see Appendix p. 142) except for:
l. 2 <racketted> cancelled for 'racketed'; l. 8 <pain> to 'pained' and
<crunch> to 'crunched' amended in IR's hand; l. 9 <clenched>
cancelled for 'shut'; l. 17 <last.> for 'last!'; l. 21 <<lessto>> mistype for
<less to>, and l. 23 <<green>> mistyped for <grain>; [ll. 20–23 <Now
let the seasons know . . . > omitted in *PPIR*]; l. 24 <ings> amended in
IR's hand in 'imaginings'; l. 25 <Earth> for 'Earth!' amended in IR's
hand; ll. 29–30 <Emptied of all that made it more than the world/In its
small fleshy compass> cancelled for 'Emptied of God-ancestralled
essences' in *PPIR*; l. 33 <<pass>> for <pass,> amended in IR's hand,
['pass' in *PPIR*]; [lines 39–47 <the air is loud with death> in *PPIR*
omitted in this TS]; l. 44 <<Maniac Earth . . . .'>> for <Maniac Earth!>
amended in IR's hand; [<Maniac Earth . . . .> lines 44–50 omitted in
PPIR]; l. 51 <on,> for 'on' ; l. 53 <its load> to 'their load' in *PPIR*; l. 63
'have' inserted after 'motion' in *PPIR*; l. 69 <blood dazed> for 'blood-
dazed'; l. 73 <<*sight*>> amended for <<brains>> in IR's hand ['sight' in

PPIR]; l. 76 <quivering bellied> for 'quivering-bellied'; <<*mles*>> amended to 'mules' in IR's hand.

Dead Man's Dump

The plunging limbers over the shattered track
Racketted with their rusty freight,
Stuck out like many crowns of thorns,
And the rusty stakes like sceptres old
To stay the flood of brutish men   5
Upon our brothers dear.

The wheels lurched over sprawled dead
But **pained** them not, though their bones **crunched**,
Their **clenched** mouths made no moan,
They lie there huddled, friend and foeman,   10
Man born of man, and born of woman,
And shells go crying over them
From night till night and now.

Earth has waited for them
All the time of their growth   15
Fretting for their decay:
Now she has them at **last**.
In the strength of their strength
Suspended – stopped and held.

Now let the seasons know   20
There are some less to feed of them
That winter need not hoard her snow
Nor autumn her fruits and green.

What fierce imaginings their dark souls lit
Earth. Have they gone into you?   25
Somewhere they must have gone,
And flung on your hard back

Is their soul's sack,
Emptied of all that made it more than the world
In its small fleshy compass   30
Who hurled them out? Who hurled?

None saw their spirits' shadow shake the grass,
Or stood aside for the half used life to **pass,**
Out of those doomed nostrils and the doomed mouth,
When the swift iron burning bee   35
Drained the wild honey of their youth.

What of us, who flung on the shrieking pyre,
Walk, our usual thoughts untouched,
Our lucky limbs as on ichor fed,
Immortal seeming ever,   40
Perhaps when the flames beat loud on us,
A fear may choke in our veins
And the startled blood may stop.

Maniac Earth! howling and flying, your bowel
Seared by the jagged fire, the iron love,   45
The impetuous storm of savage love.
Dark Earth! Dark heaven, swinging in chemic smoke
What dead are born when you kiss each soundless soul
With lightning and thunder from your mined heart,
Which man's self dug, and his blind fingers loosed.   50

A man's brains splattered **on,**
A stretcher-bearer's face;
His shook shoulders slipped **its load,**
But when they bent to look again
The drowning soul was sunk too deep   55
For human tenderness.
They left this dead with the older dead,
Stretched at the cross roads.

Burnt black by strange decay
Their sinister faces lie   60
The lid over each eye,
The grass and coloured clay
More motion than they,
Joined to the great sunk silences.

Here is one not long dead,   65
His dark hearing caught our far wheels,
And the choked soul stretched weak hands,
To reach the living word the far wheels said,
The **blood dazed** intelligence beating for light,
Crying through the suspense of the far-torturing wheels,   70
Swift for the end to break,
Or the wheels to break,
Cried as the tide of the world broke over his **brains.**

Will they come? Will they ever come?
Even as the mixed hoofs of the mules,   75
The **quivering bellied mules,**
And the rushing wheels all mixed,
With his tortured upturned sight
So we crashed round the bend,
We heard his weak scream,   80
We heard his very last sound,
And our wheels grazed his dead face.

P. Fragment pencil holograph in Rosenberg's hand (mislettered N by Bottomley) including underlined heading and punctuation on torn scrap of paper enclosed with letter P (mislettered N by Bottomley) above. As in *PPIR* except: ll. 3–5 <Emptied of all that made the young lean Time . . . > cancelled for 'Emptied of God-ancestralled essences.'; l. 6 <hurld> for 'hurled'. **Unpublished variant.**

From line 26 'Dead man's dump altered *

And flung on your hard back
Is their soul's sack
Emptied of all that made the young lean Time
Eye with thief's eyes, shouldering his masters* load
Of proud Godhead ancestralled essences   5
Who hurled them out? Who hurld?

Qa. Letter to Bottomley with envelope dated from postmark 3 August
1917. Poem opening as printed in *PPIR*, p. 142 (see Appendix p. 140)
except for: l. 1 <knows> for 'beats', <limbs> for 'limbs-'; l. 3 <Here>
omitted; [additional line after l. 3 in *PPIR*]; l. 4 <side shut> for 'and
shut' in *PPIR*; l. 7 <<*failed*>> crossed out for <expiring> by IR; [lines
<5–7> omitted, 9 lines added, in *PPIR*]. Part published *CW*79, p. 260.
Unpublished paragraphs.

My Dear Mr Bottomley
Do you think this a better opening for my 'Daughters of War'

Space knows the ruddy freedom of their limbs
Their naked dances with mans spirit naked
Here by the root side of the tree of life
(Side shut from earth's profoundest eyes)
Their shining dances beckon our dumb faces   5
⎰ Before the pierced voice has ceased in the tree tops ⎱
⎱ Before the expiring voice has ceased in the boughs? ⎰
The old bark burnt with iron wars &c

I think it makes the poem clearer for I hate to think my idea is lost as
it must be if the expression is uncertain. Now Mr Marsh wants to
print my 'Kolue'* speech in Moses for the Georgian book,[†] but I am
certain my most epic poem, so far, is the Daughters poem, but it is

* [sic]
† *Georgian Poetry 1916-17*, vol. 3, op. cit., p. 53.

too obscure, he thinks. I believe if one gets hold of the opening it should be easy enough to follow. Where do you think the poem is obscure [sic]

I don't think I'll get my play complete for it in time; though it ill [sic] hardly take much space, it's so slight. If I could get home on leave I'd work at it and get it done, no doubt, but leaves are so chancy. It's called 'The Unicorn.' Now, it's about a decaying race who have never seen as woman; animals take the place of women, but they yearn for continuity. The chief's Unicorn breaks away and he goes in chase. The Unicorn is found by boys outside a city and brought in, and breaks away again. Saul, who has seen the Unicorn on his way to the city for the week's victuals, gives chase in his cart. A storm comes on, the mules break down, and by the lightning he sees the Unicorn race by; a naked black like an apparition rises up and easily lifts the wheels from the rut, and together they ride to Saul's hut. There Lilith is in great consternation, having seen the Unicorn, and knowing the legend of this race of men.

The emotions of the black (the chief) are the really difficult part of my story. Afterwards <the> [crossed out] a host of blacks on horses, like centaurs and buffaloes, come rushing up, [sic] the Unicorn in front. On every horse is clasped a woman. Lilith faints, Saul stabs himself, the Chief places Lilith on the Unicorn, and they all race away.

I hope you're keeping that pleasantness of condition your last letter showed.

Yours sincerely

Isaac Rosenberg.

Ill [sic] send bits of the play when I get it into some shape

Q1. Fragment pencil holograph. Unpublished.
I sent the latter part of this letter & forgot this.

Q2. Envelope addressed to Bottomley postmarked 3 August 1917.

R1. Letter to Bottomley with envelope dated from postmark 19 August 1917.

(NB *CW79* p. 257 includes R1 as being to Edward Marsh 17 June 1917 but from the MS letter it is clearly to Bottomley, 19 August 1917). Part published in *CW79*, p. 257. **Unpublished paragraphs.**

Dear Mr Bottomley

Please do not trouble to answer my letters as I am sure it is difficult to write when you are not well. I cannot say how much I feel your taking to my writings, & how I hate to think of you in pain. Does not the open air relieve you, & walking? I will continue to write even if I know my letter helped to make a nice cup of tea, and was the very basis of the fire.

I am now fearfully rushed, but find energy enough to scribble this in the minute I plunder from my work. I believe I can see the obscurities in the 'Daughters,' but hardly hope to clear them up in France. The first part, the picture of the Daughters dancing and calling to the spirits of the slain before their last cries have ceased among the boughs of the tree of life, I must still work on. In that part obscure the description of the voice of the Daughter I have not made clear, <the earth> [crossed out] I see; I have tried to suggest the wonderful sound of her voice, spiritual and voluptuous at the same time. The end is an attempt to imagine the severance of all human relationship and the fading away of human love. Later on I will try and work on it, because I think it a pity if the ideas are to be lost for want of work.

My 'Unicorn' play is stopped because of my increased toil, and I forget how much or little I told you of it, I want to do it in one Act, although I think I have a subject here that could make a gigantic play. I have not the time to write out the sketch of it as far as it's gone, though I'd like to know your criticism of it very much.

The difficult part I shrink from; I think even Shakespeare might, the first time Tel, the chief of the decaying race, sees a woman (who is Lilith, Saul's wife), and he is called upon to talk. Saul and Lilith are ordinary folk into whose ordinary lives the unicorn bursts. It is to be a play of terror—terror of hidden things and the fear of the supernatural.

But I see no hope of doing the play while out here. I have a way, when I write, of trying to put myself in the situation, and I make gestures and grimaces. <and I don't want to risk being> [crossed out] **We are fearfully busy now & it has been an effort to write this letter but your letters always give me great delight, & I must let you know.**
Yours sincerely
Isaac Rosenberg.

R2. Letter to Bottomley, ink, dated in Bottomley's hand Sept 21 1917. Enclosed in blank envelope inscribed in Bottomley's hand 'On leave September 1917'. Some full stops missing in final 5 lines. Part published in *CW79*, p. 262. **Unpublished paragraphs.**

87 Dempsey St
Stepney London E

Dear Mr Bottomley
The greatest thing of my leave after seeing my mother was your letter which has just arrived. **I am sure you are happy now or you could not have anyway, written that letter.** <it is> [crossed out] I wish I could have seen you, but now I must go on and hope that things will turn out well, and some happy day will give me the chance of meeting you. **I waited to write till this because I wanted you to see my idea of the 'Unicorn' my sister has been typing for you.** I am afraid I can do no writing or reading; I feel so restless here and un-anchored. We have lived in such an elemental way so long, things here don't look quite right to me somehow; or it may be the conciousness [sic] of my so limited time here for freedom – so little time to do so many things – bewilders me. <if the>[crossed out] 'The Unicorn', as will be obvious, is just a <nuclear> [crossed out] basis; its final form will be very different, I hope. **But the story is sketched out. Tell me if it appears trashy; I <will>** [crossed out] **have no feeling at all about it just now, and I am anxious to hear yours – if its** [sic] **suggestions are clear to you of course. My queer situation makes me send it in a state like that as you will understand. One never knows**

whether one gets the chance again of writing. It happens my younger brother is on leave as well now, & brother-in-law, & all my people are pretty lively & won't let me isolate myself to write <though> [crossed out]; Mr Trevelyan sent me his comedy I think it is very fine for what it is meant – I had very great pleasure from it [sic] A little more of that kind of thing might bring people to their senses. I am taking it back to France with me. I am sending a Photograph of myself happy in Blighty. I wish you could send one of yours. If I can find the 'Adam & Eve' picture I told you of I'll send that before I go back.

Yours sincerely
Isaac Rosenberg.

My mother & my sister tell me to thank you for the pleasure your letters to me give them. They thank you for your friendliness – I thank you for something more.

R3. Letter to Bottomley, marked in Bottomley's hand '1.15pm 25 Sept 1917.' Unpublished.

87 Dempsey St
Stepney E London

Dear Mr Bottomley
I think you will be ammused [sic] at these things enclosed. I send three because each is different. The chap with me is my very young brother and I am in civvies again. The suit & the hat is the family suit & hat, & fits us all, [sic] though my younger brother is growing out of it now. Your letter about my 'Unicorn' is much better than my 'unicorn' itself. You have taken a lot of trouble to go over it & it makes me believe in it. You have got my idea of it exactly as I have, & your scheme of amplification I had in mind as well, but you have put it down so excellently & consise [sic] and more coherently realised. You know how impossible it it to work it out, placed as I am – if I had been an officer I might have managed it,

but we Tommies are too full up. I have other copies of those <things> [crossed out] poems I sent so don't trouble to return them. We have been to one theatre & nearly got turned out for giving expression to our feelings about it; we have been to no more. I see friends & go from one place to another & feel fearfully restless. I cannot read. But this is a great change: one can also get properly clean again and begin afresh. My 'Adam & Eve' I cannot find anywhere but if I come across it before I go I will send it. I hope very much youre [sic] getting the very best out of your holiday,

Isaac Rosenberg.

I go back Thursday

Isaac Rosenberg in 'the family suit & hat' with his youngest brother Elkon in uniform, inscribed by IR 'G. Bottomley from Isaac Rosenberg 1917' (R3 to Bottomley, p. 107). Credit: Imperial War Museum. Photographic Archive IWM Doc 759.

R4. **Lettercard to Bottomley,** ink, dated 28 September 1917.
Unpublished.

> 87 Dempsey St
> Stepney E

Dear Mr Bottomley

After missing about three days [sic] trains I am off again to France
now. I hope you have not sent that photo you promised to France
because I hear we're shifted up to Belgium & your letter may
miscarry. If you are sending, send it to my people & they will
forward it. Have left < sending > [crossed out] instructions to send
drawing

> IR.

S. **Letter to Bottomley** with envelope dated from two postmarks:
16 October 1917 & 'Carnforth Army Post Office 13 October 1917'; written
upside down on headed notepaper 'YMCA On Active Service with
the British Expeditionary Force'. **Unpublished.**

> 22311 Pte I Rosenberg
> 11 KORL attached 229 Field Coy RE
> Ward B.6.
> 51 general [sic] Hospital BEF France

Dear Mr Bottomley

When I returned from my holiday I was taken sick and sent down
the line. So I can write to you more leisurely than before. When I
was in England I felt too restless to write or read; but I went round
and made some purchases & one, or two rather, was your Chambers
of Imagery.* I brought the first series back with me and reread it.
If there was a book that tantalised; if there ever was a pleasure
that annoyed one – its [sic] your book. Like enjoying some fascinat-
ing phenomena through glasses; suddenly the glasses are broken
& you can see no more. There are <were>[crossed out] far too few

---

* Gordon Bottomley, *Chambers of Imagery,* op. cit., see p. 93.

poems in the book. Every one is astonishing but the book is too brief. Of course I know your work is spread about in other books, but I had not your other books near me at the time.

The little poem 'Tanagra' I once enjoyed so much I read again with just the same pleasure. 'Sailors' is a bit difficult – the last verse is very very fine & the opening pictures of the poem are gorgeous. When I returned I found your letter of Sept 19 for me. It is a beautiful letter and I am very glad it was not lost. I am most glad in that I have been mistaken about your pains. I was told you were in continual suffering – & it is as good to me as the war being over to hear otherwise, from yourself. I don't know whether you sent that photo you promised – whether it will yet reach me, or has got lost, but I am looking forward to seeing it very much. If ever I get the chance I will remind you of your promise to sit for me – if I still have the skill and power to draw. I wrote a small poem I'll enclose. I may now be able to think about my unicorn although so many things happening puts [sic] all ideas out of ones head.

Yours sincerely
I Rosenberg.

S. Holograph poem 'Girl to Soldier' enclosed with letter S, on blue paper; as in *PPIR*, p. 145 (see Appendix p. 145) except for: <'Girl to Soldier> for 'Girl to Soldier on Leave' title; l. 1 <you,Titan> for 'you-Titan'; l. 2 <storm days> for 'storm-days'; l. 3 <sons> for 'son'; l. 4 <whom I should> for 'who I would'; l. 5 <Pallid day,> for 'Pallid days'; [additional verses ll. 5–8 & 16–20 in *PPIR*]; l. 7 <wings> for 'tops'; l. 8 <Bore down> for 'Pressed'; l. 9 <Vulturelike> for 'Weary gyves'; l. 13 <me, your> for 'me-your'.

Girl to Soldier

I love **you,** Titan lover,
My own **storm days** Titan.
Greater than the **sons** of Zeus,
I know **whom I should** choose.

Pallid days, arid & wan   5
Tied your soul fast,
Babel cities smoky **wings**
Bore down on your growth.
Vulturelike . . . what were you?
But a word in the brain's ways   10
Or the sleep of Circe's swine,
One gyve holds you yet.

Love! You love **me,** your eyes
Have looked through death at mine.
You have tempted a grave too much.   15
I let you – I repine.

T. **Letter to Bottomley** with envelope dated from postmark 22 October 1917. **Unpublished.**

22311 Pt I Rosenberg
11th KORL attd 229 Field Coy RE
Lines B6 51 General Hospital BEF

Dear Mr Bottomley

I enclose a poem Ive [sic] just written – its [sic] sad enough I know – but one can hardly write a war poem & be anything else. It happened to one of our chaps poor fellow – and I've tried to write it. My sister wrote me you had rec [sic] our unlucky & ancient Adam & Eve; I hope it is not too badly damaged. It was suggested to me by a poem of Verhaven* [sic] I read in English, where Adam and Eve rushed together. I heard from Mr Trevelyan who tells me he is near you. < Some more > [crossed out] I found a vol of F Thompsons [sic] poems here and some of his poems are as good as anything in our language. But I don't like him as I did the first time I read him – he is much too fond of stars. But the Fallen Yew, A Judgement in Heaven

---

*   Emile Verhaeren (1855–1916), Belgian poet and playwright.

the hymn to the Setting Sun* [sic] – & a few more – are equal to any poems written. I do hope for that time to come when I shall be free to read and write in my own time; there will be the worries again of earning a livelyhood [sic]; painting is a very unsatisfactory business; but I can teach – though after the life I have lived in the army I don't think it would matter much to me what I did. I will write again soon.

Yours sincerely

Isaac Rosenberg.

T. **Holograph poem 'In War'** in pencil upside down on headed note-paper 'YMCA On Active Service with British Expeditionary Force' enclosed with letter T above; as in *PPIR*, p. 131 (see Appendix p. 146) except for: l. 2, 3 & 4 <thy> for 'your'; l. 16 <<*voice*>> crossed out by IR for 'ghost'; l. 28 <suns> for 'sun's'; l. 44 <irrevelant> for 'irrelevant'; l. 46 <I heard> for 'I heard'.

In War

Fret the nonchalant noon
With **thy** spleen
Or **thy** gay brow,
For the motion of **thy** spirit
Ever moves with these.   5

When day shall be too quiet,
Deaf to you
And your dumb smile,
Untuned air shall lap the stillness
In the old space for your **voice** –   10

The voice that once could mirror
Remote depths

* Francis Thompson, 'A Fallen Yew', p. 43; 'A Judgement in Heaven', p. 58; 'Ode to the Setting Sun', p. 205, *The Collected Poetry* (London: Hodder & Stoughton, 1913).

Of moving being,
Stirred by responsive voices near,
Suddenly stilled for ever.   15

No <<*voice*>> ghost darkens the places
Dark to One;
But my eyes dream,
And my heart is heavy to think
How it was heavy once.   20

In the old days when death
Stalked the world
For the flower of men,
And the rose of beauty faded
And pined in the great gloom,   25

One day we dug a grave:
We were vexed
With the **suns** heat.
We scanned the hooded dead:
At noon we sat & talked   30

How death had kissed their eyes
Three dread noons since,
How human art won
The dark soul to flicker
Till it was lost again.   35

And we whom chance kept whole –
But haggard,
Spent, were charged
To make a place for them who knew
No pain in any place.   40

The good priest came to pray:
Our ears half heard,
And half we thought
Of alien things, **irrevelant** [sic];
And the heat & thirst were great.   45

The good priest read: **I heard** . . .
Dimly my brain
Held words and lost . . .
Suddenly my blood ran cold . . .
God! God! It could not be.   50

He read my brother's name;
I sank –
I clutched the priest.
They did not tell me it was he
Was killed three days ago.   55
What are the great sceptred dooms
To us, caught
In the wild wave?
We break ourselves on them,
My brother, our hearts and years.   60

U. **Letter to Bottomley** dated from postmark ? (illegible) October 1917.
Unpublished.

22311 Pte I Rosenberg
11th KORL attd 229 field Coy RE
Lines B6 51 General Hospital BEF France

Dear Mr Bottomley
Though I am denying myself enormous pleasure I feel sure, I want
to stop you from sending your book out to me – it will only get lost
& if I knew I could buy it again afterwards of course I should not be
so troubled about it. It is a pleasure to be saved up for me & I thank

115

you very much for this. I believe I am a great tax on your time & invention with my correspondence; however while you do not say so, & give such wonderful exchange for my rubbish, I will go on. I was sorry at the news of your last letter indeed, & don't know what to say – so much sadness is happening in these terrible times that one is either bewildered or becomes insensible. I brought your 'Chambers of Imagery'* out with me when I first came out but it vanished as well as Emerson's poems. If you really like the 'Adam & Eve' I am well satisfied with it. I have another at home called the Family of Adam which you must see some time. Now your photo – I do wish I had the chance to paint you. I think Id do a memorable work – you hardly look an invalid from the photo – I hope all that is an exploded myth. So that is Edward Thomas.† I used to read his criticisms & thought them very sound & intelligent; but I know very little else of his work. I have been thinking of my Unicorn & your suggestions.

I want to open with the tower of sculls [sic] of the decaying men. An ancient hermaphrodite is about to die & tells the secret of their birth. Tel the chief the rider of the unicorn plans the raid, I have been reading Shakespeare here, the comedies, & can see how hampered he was by a public, though no doubt that also impelled him to work out clearly a large idea. But I fancy Browning – say in Pippa Passes had in mind certain weaknesses, & giving way to the public of Shakespeare & worked out a more interesting form, though no one can touch Shakespeare for masterly handling & illuminating grasp of character & motives.

Now I should like to write my play in prose a good deal & where it becomes vehement, poetry. As I write it, if I can think of anything, I will get it typed, but it will hardly be fair to you if I let you see it, till it is <pretty much> [crossed out by IR] more welded together & riper for a verdict.

---

* Gordon Bottomley, *Chambers of Imagery*, op. cit., see p. 93.
† Edward Thomas, poet and critic, and a friend of Bottomley's, was killed at the Battle of Arras in April 1917. It seems that the photograph of himself which Bottomley sent Rosenberg may have also included Edward Thomas, and that the 'news' of his letter was of Thomas's death some months before.

I am lucky, true, to be here in this poor weather, but it may not be long before Im [sic] out – I cannot say though.

Yours sincerely

Isaac Rosenberg.

V. Letter to Bottomley dated from postmark 'Field Post Office 30 Jan 1918', in Bottomley's hand. **Unpublished.**

Dear Mr Bottomley

I have been in the trenches some time now & it is most awkward to get letters away, <but> [crossed out by IR] **I had the Georgian Book*** sent me & though I had to send it back I had just time to gallop through it & seeing yours made me very anxious to know what has been happening to you. There are some things in the GB that delight me as much as anything – JC Squire's 'house' is fine & one or two more things. Your 'Atlantis' gives the book a first class quality & it is a pity Abercrombie has nothing. My address is

Pte I Rosenberg 22311

4 platoon A. Coy

11th KORL BEF

Im [sic] writing this in the line & have no light or paper. There is a lot I'd like to write – [line blocked out by censors] I have Balzacean schemes suggested this time. I just write this to let you know Im still a harrassed [sic] mortal. IR

W. Letter to Bottomley with envelope, dated by Rosenberg Feb 17th; 1918 added in Bottomley's hand (postmarked 19 Feb). **Unpublished.**

Feb 17th

Dear Mr Bottomley

I do not know when I begin a letter whether to plunge <right to the depths> [crossed out] **into gloomiest of Byronic misanthropy (as**

---

* *Georgian Poetry 1916–17*, op. cit., see p. 26.

indeed, my inclination pushes me to,) or be nice and placid & acquiescent about things. I know if I didn't explain myself properly Id [sic] only appear weak & stupid, & as the situation does not give me the chance to explain myself, it must be left unexplained just yet, at least. From your letter, <inexplicable> [crossed out] your cause of complaint has been most real & that you have been able to write to me is, I hope, a true sign that all is over. I am delighted that you are writing poetry again – it is too long since youve [sic] written. I liked 'New Years Eve'. It perhaps had not the richness & exceptional effect of the others – but it had the qualities you aimed for – piercing & vital. I have been transfered [sic] to Pte I Rosenberg 22311 8 Platoon, B Coy, 1st Batt KORL BEF. My own Batt is broken up & what was left of them mixed up with other Battalions. Just now we are out for a 'rest'. Poetry seems to have gone right out of me I get no chance to even think of it. My 'Unicorn' is dead, & it will need a powerful Messiah to breathe life into its nostrils. I could more easily draw than write but the weather is too cold for that, if I did get the time. Thank you for what you say about my 'Kolue' [sic] speech. If the war does not damage me completely Ill [sic] beat that yet.

Yours sincerely
Isaac Rosenberg.

X. Letter to Bottomley with envelope postmarked 26 Feb 1918 on notepaper headed: Church Army Recreation Hut, dated by Rosenberg 24 Feb; 1918 added in Bottomley's hand; published *CW79*, p. 268. Unpublished paragraphs.

Dear Mr Bottomley

I am still on rest; it may be only for a while. When I get up the line again it is goodbye to letter writing for a dreary time; unless one writes from hospital soon. <Even now> [crossed out] I know a letter that is not expressive is hardly worth sending, but yet from the seat of war any kind of letter means a lot – if it only implies security. I wanted to send some bits I wrote for 'The Unicorn', while

I was in hospital, and if I find them I'll enclose them. I tried to work on your suggestion and divided it into 4 acts, but since I left the hosp. all poetry has gone quite out of me. I seem even to forget works, and I believe if I met anybody with ideas I'd be dumb. No drug could be more stupifying [sic] than our work (to me anyway), and this goes on like that old torture of water trickling, drop by drop unendingly <until> [crossed out] on one's helplessness.

Pte I **Rosenberg** 22311 8 Platoon B Coy 1st Batt, <11th> [crossed out] **KORL BEF. I find I can't copy these bits from the Unicorn so am sending one or two poor things, but I aimed for something in them.**

X. **Holograph poem** enclosed with above letter X. As in *PPIR*, p. 273 (see Appendix p. 146) except for: title; <piled up> for 'piled-up'; l. 9 <<*is less*>> [crossed out by IR]; l. 10 <scull> for 'skulls'; l. 6 <deaths> for 'death's'; l. 17 <walk> for 'walls'.

From the Unicorn

The Tower of *Sculls* [sic]

Mourners
These layers of **piled up** skulls, –
These layers of gleaming horror – stark horror.
Ah me! Through my thin hands they touch my eyes.

Everywhere, everywhere is a pregnant birth,   5
And here in **deaths** land is a pregnant birth.
Your own crying is less mortal
Than the amazing soul in your body.

Your own crying <<*is less*>> yon parrot takes up
And from your empty **scull** cries it afterwards.   10

Thou whose dark activities unenchanted
Days from gyrating days, suspending them

To thrust them far from sight, from the gyrating days
Which have gone widening on & left us here,
Cast derelicts lost for ever.   15

When aged flesh looks down on tender brood;
For he knows between his thin ribs **walk**
The giant universe, the interminable
Panorama – synods, myths and creeds,
He knows his dust is fire and seed.   20

X cont. Holograph poem enclosed with letter X above. As printed in
PPIR, p. 130 (see Appendix p. 149) except: title <dying> for 'Dying';
l. 7 <!> omitted.

The *dying* Soldier

'Here are houses' he moaned,
'I could reach but my brain swims'.
Then they thundered and flashed
And shook the earth to its rims.

'They are gunpits' he gasped,   5
'Our men are at the guns.
Water ... water ... O! water
For one of England's dying sons'.

We cannot give you water
Were all England in your breath'.   10
'Water! ... Water! ... O! Water!'
He moaned and swooned to death.

X cont. Typescript poem 'The burning of the Temple' enclosed with
letter X above. As printed in *PPIR*, p. 147 (see Appendix p. 149). except
for: l. 9 <?> omitted.

The Burning of the Temple

Fierce wrath of Solomon
Where sleepest thou? O see
The fabric which thou won
Earth and ocean to give thee –
O look at the red skies.   5

Or hath the sun plunged down?
What is this molten gold –
These thundering fires blown
Through heaven – where the smoke rolled.
Again the great king dies.   10

His dreams go out in smoke,
His days he let not pass
And sculptured here are broke
Are charred as the burnt grass
Gone as his mouth's last sighs.   15

X cont. Typescript poem 'Returning, we hear the larks' enclosed
with letter X above. As printed in *PPIR*, p. 138 (see Appendix p. 150)
except: l. 5 <poison blasted> for 'poison-blasted'; l. 9 <listning> for
'list'ning'.

Returning, we hear the larks

Sombre the night is.
And though we have our lives, we know
What sinister threat lurks there.

Dragging these anguished limbs, we only know
This **poison blasted** track opens on our camp –   5
On a little safe sleep.

But hark! joy – joy – strange joy.
Lo! heights of night ringing with unseen larks.
Music showering our upturned **listning** faces.

Death could drop from the dark   10
As easily as song –
But song only **dropped,**
Like a blind man's dreams on the sand
By dangerous tides,
Like a girl's dark hair for she dreams no ruin lies there,   15
Or her kisses where a serpent hides.

Y. Letter to Bottomley with envelope postmarked 9 Mar 1918 on
notepaper headed: Church Army Recreation Hut, dated by Rosenberg
7 March 1918, *CW*79, p. 269. **Unpublished paragraphs.**

Dear Mr Bottomley
I believe our interlude is nearly over, & we may go up the line any
moment now, so I answer your letter straightaway. If only this war were
over our eyes would not be on death so much; – it seems to underlie
even our underthoughts. Yet when I have been as near to it as anybody
could be, the idea has never crossed my mind – certainly not so
much as when some lying doctor told me I had consumption. I like
to think of myself as a poet; so what you say, though I know it to be
extravagant, gives me immense pleasure.

**Your six horse metaphor is very kind & gratifying criticism &
you may be sure I will keep it in mind. In the page for 'The Unicorn'
they were disconnected bits Id** [sic] **selected from some poorer stuff
so I am sorry for puzzling you.** < 'several of our chaps living at ?
Warrington . . . are going on leave. I'll try and send ac . . .> [Lines
cancelled by censor but largely legible.]

I am trying to get transfered [sic] **to the 'Judaens'. I think they
are now in Mesopotamia. Jacob Epstein whom I know is with the
Judaens & several other friends of mine. They also run a magazine.**

If I ever do get the chance to run up to Warrington & it is not at all unlikely for the situation you've imaged out to happen very shortly, Id [sic] jump at the chance: I don't think Ive [sic] a chance of leave for a long long time, or I might go then. We hear a lot of this coming earthquake along the line; but whatever happens if I can, I will always write you, & keep you informed of my existence.

Yours sincerely Isaac Rosenberg.

9 Platoon B coy 1st KORL BEF France

Do you see Mr Trevelyan. I think I told you Id [sic] read his Farce* in the war & how deeply true it was. He has the sentiments of most of us out here. Above all I am most glad to [sic] in your note of hope & confidence – one of my great peacetime pleasures must be to read a new play of yours.

---

* R. C. Trevelyan, *The Pterodamozels*, a comedy (1916), *Collected Poems* (London: Longmans Green, 1939), p. 179.

Letters and memoirs written to Laurence Binyon

The following memoirs and letters were written to Laurence Binyon by Rosenberg's sister, his correspondents, and others who had known him, in connection with the preparation of *Poems by Isaac Rosenberg* (PR22), selected and edited by Gordon Bottomley with an introductory memoir by Laurence Binyon. **All are unpublished except Annie Wynick's *Memoir*, first published in *Art and Letters* (London: Summer 1919).**

1. Letter to Binyon from Gordon Bottomley, in ink dated 30th June 1919.

> The Sheiling
> Silverdale
> Near Carnforth

My dear Binyon

I think perhaps you will be back in Town by now, so I send with this my bundle of Rosenberg letters again, about which you asked.

I have been looking up the Pozières poem, in which Eddie [Edward Marsh] questioned 'This monstrous girth of glory, this marvellous glory', saying he thought these were alternatives and that one should be cancelled.

The only copy of this poem is in the letter to me of August 29th 1916, marked 'E' in the bundle [see Letter E, p. 82]. On referring to it I find that the verses look very much like a fair copy made for the purpose of including in the letter, as they look preternaturally tidy for Rosenberg. The line in question seems to be arranged thus deliberately and there seems to me to be good reason to believe that he meant both phrases to stand and that he liked the rhetorical device.

I wonder if you could spare my collection of R's poems just now? If you can I think it might be best for me to go over it and make the necessary emendations while Eddie's suggestions are fresh in my mind; and I should also like to shew [sic] it to [Lascelles] Abercrombie (who is staying in the village for the next two months and is writing the most topping things imaginable). He knew Rosenberg before I did, but has not seen the later things.

I still read your letter about my plays every day, and each time I am full of glory and renew my thanks.

Ever Yours

Gordon Bottomley.

2. Letter to Binyon from Gordon Bottomley, in ink dated 5 July 1919.

The Sheiling

Silverdale

Near Carnforth

My Dear Binyon

I have been considerably astonished to receive the enclosed by this afternoon's post.

I suppose the irrepressible and indefatigable Semitess [Annie Rosenberg] can do what she likes with her brother's poems; but I feel she ought not to entrust them to you and to me and then go behind us like this. It is not fair, and may weaken the appeal of the book.

For her action seems to me to imply one of two things; either

(i) She did not hand over the whole of her material to us; in which case I may have been prevented from making the selection as good as possible; or

(ii) She has kept duplicates of the typed copies I got her to make; in which case she may have handed over to Mr Schiff [Sydney Schiff] the results of my editorial labour and painful deciphering – which would be just a little vexatious.

I should have suspected her of wanting to make as much money as possible by handing over the poems to two parties at once in this way; but I doubt if *Art and Letters* pays enough to make that a probable theory.

It may be just her artless and naïve desire to do the best she can for her brother's memory. Possibly, too, it may not matter very much except in principle; but she ought to be warned not to accept people's help and then go behind them in this way, oughtn't she? Or she may do it more than once and make the book a nullity.

So I thought I would send you this line to ask what you think ought to be done – I have not replied to Mr S. Schiff, and I shall do nothing until I hear from you.[*]

Many thanks for the MS safely to hand, and for your sending it so soon. Abercrombie sends his remembrances, and his congratulations, which he was delighted to have. He is working again, *Laus Deo*, and more splendidly than ever before – his powers have gathered together in the silent interval, and his sense of form is tremendously widened.

In much haste for the post, your

GB

3. **Letter to Binyon from Frank Emanuel,** in ink dated 28 April 1921.

> 2 St Johns Gardens
> Holland Park
> XI

Dear Sir

In response to a communication from Mrs Wynick I went to see her yesterday re the book about her brother which I hear is being compiled. I am glad to hear that it is being undertaken – and the more so that it is in such distinguished and sympathetic hands.

---

[*] Annie Wynick, née Rosenberg, was an indefatigable supporter of her brother's work, and it was her determination which preserved so much of it. It was undoubtedly only because she was unfamiliar with the conventions of publication that she approached more than one publisher at the same time. The problem, such as it was, was speedily resolved and Sydney Schiff printed her *Memoir* (below, p. 133) together with five poems and a pencil study by Rosenberg in the periodical he edited and published, *Art and Letters* (London: Summer 1919). In the same edition Schiff also publicised the 1922 edition (PR22).

I took her a very beautiful drawing of a barrister done in red chalk by Rosenberg to which I awarded a prize at one of the monthly meetings of 'The Limners' which for some fifteen years used to meet at my studio or house for criticism or chat. I purchased the drawing from young Rosenberg.

Mrs Wynick was very anxious that I should write you [sic] about my knowledge of her brother as I had been his guardian (Jewish Bd. of Guardians) during the period that he was an apprentice. As an apprentice the poor chap always chafed against being in trade – although of course as in all such cases an *art* trade in which his ability would at any rate have *some* play was found for him. I pointed out to him how difficult it was for an artist – even provided with certain means – to earn a living as a painter and urged him first to learn an art trade – to fall back upon – so that in case of need he would not be destitute. Meanwhile he was encouraged to push forward his art on all *available* occasions so as to reach a point at which he would be justified on abandoning trade and launching out.

'The Limners' was a body of artists and art teachers who were trusting enough to listen to my criticism of their work. I gave them prizes of prints and such like – found little jobs for some of them now and then and had exhibitions to which the public came and purchased in my studio and elsewhere – I felt that it was an opportunity to bring East and West end together and under the mutual interest of art to foster such social intercourse as would lessen class feeling. For Rosenberg whose circumstances had rendered him very bitter and despondent I felt to become a member would be a good thing and I got him and several other East End artists enrolled. I took care to give him and others like him and others like placed special encouragement and consideration. Later as you will know he did not lack the kind friendship of those who could and did help him very materially. Unfortunately Rosenberg had not the knack of showing to those who went out of their way to help him – that he appreciated their efforts. Though I understand he wrote a poem to Amschewitz who was extremely kind to him as he was to others.

I always regretted that (with the sole desire of helping him) certain of his friends decided to send him to the Slade School – at this time enveloped in an extremely nasty and unhealthy 'atmosphere'. The art produced there was morbid, artificial and unclean and that influence has not yet dissipated itself. The influence was bad for any young artist and doubly so for the already socialistic East End boys, who really required fresh air and sunshine let into their work and their lives to make their lives and their achievements healthier and happier. At the Slade stage scenery was preferred to nature, ugliness, sordidness and disease were preferred in its models – to beauty and health and cleanliness.

The results of these surroundings were soon traceable in Rosenberg's art work – as in that of so many others who had started with less brilliant promise than he – at least so it seemed to me.

Later I saw Rosenberg very infrequently, he left the Limners – but I heard of him by enquiry from mutual friends. He certainly was a remarkably clever young fellow and I can't help thinking – a great poet. I believe that therein lay his greater strength, his beauty of written language astounds me.

It is a thousand pities that he did not live to see those better circumstances that would very likely have softened and sweetened his outlook on life.

His joining up and his war record I regard as simply *heroic*. He was physically such a weakling though mentally so exceptionally well-equipped.

Apologies for the too-personal note in these views believe me dear Sir

Yours truly
Frank Emanuel

2. Letter to Binyon from Winifreda Seaton, in ink dated 18 November 1919.

> 62 Milton Park
> Highgate
> N6

Dear Mr Binyon

I should not have troubled you at all, but I wrote to Mr Bottomley (not however sending any letters) suggesting he might like to see the correspondence, and I had no reply. Later, I saw in *Art and Letters** that you were helping him. I've no doubt he thought I was the usual irritating female trying to get into prominence by clinging to the tail of Mr Rosenberg's Pegasus.

Thank you very much for so kindly receiving my letter. According to my own impressions you are absolutely right in your judgement of his poetic gift. He died too soon, which cannot be said of Sir Philip Sidney or Keats with the same deep regret. Had he had Rupert Brooke's advantages he might have expressed himself more perfectly, but when you can you compare the environment of the two, Isaac Rosenberg is a wonder.

I enclose a few more letters (I think these even more illuminating than the others) which I found in one of my old diaries. You can see in them his consciousness of the difficulties he had in his way. He grew to care for Donne almost as much as I do – like Jonson I put him first in the world for some things – and I remember a note of his beginning 'You cruel girl, what have you done with my Donne?' when I kept an old and rather curious copy he picked up somewhere, and was in the habit of looking into every day. I have a good number of Isaac Rosenberg's poems in manuscript and copied some of his earliest ones. I have no idea whether Mr Bottomley intends a complete edition or a selection, but I will gladly send any of mine to him for collation if it is worth while.

---

* *Art and Letters*, published by Sydney Schiff, op cit., see footnote to Bottomley's letter to Binyon above, p. 126.

Please don't trouble to answer this and be sure you to keep the letters until it is quite convenient for you to return them.

Yours sincerely
Winifreda Seaton.

A short prose essay on 'Realism and Imagination in Paint' is included, as he enclosed it in a letter.

[Rosenberg's letters and poems to Winifreda Seaton have not been found. Neither is this essay in the present collection; it may have been a version of his lecture 'On Modern Art' which follows his short piece 'The Pre-Raphaelites and Imagination in Paint' in *CW79*, pp. 298–9.]

5. **Letter to Binyon from Morley Dainow,** typescript on headed notepaper, dated 18 December 1920.

The Pelman Laboratory of Applied Psychology
The Pelman Institute, Ltd
Director of the Laboratory
Morley Dainow BSC (Lond)
10 Oakley House
Bloomsbury Street
London WC1
<u>Personal and Confidential</u>

Dear Sir

I am exceedingly sorry that owing to my absence from London on a lecture tour in Scotland, and owing to great pressure of scientific and business work, I have been unable to reply to your interesting letter of October 7th , about Isaac Rosenberg.

The original Ms. has been received, for which many thanks. I note that you have made a copy of the Poem and sent it to Mr. Bottomley, and I also note with pleasure that you are likely to make mention of this early poem in your introduction. Pray do so.

You ask me whether I knew Rosenberg well. At the time I was a librarian employed in the Public library at Whitechapel, and took a leading part in a Reading Circle that met once a week. My enthusiasm and useful service brought me into contact with a large number of readers who were seeking advice as to books.

One day I was approached by a Jewish young lady [Minnie Rosenberg] who asked me whether I could help her young brother whose aim in life was to be a poet. The next day a fragile Jewish boy was brought to me by this lady. This boy was Isaac Rosenberg. I took young Rosenberg for walks, and discovered him to be perfectly convinced that his vocation in life was that of a Poet and a Painter. He was then, I believe, between the ages of 10 and 12 years. I enjoyed being with the boy and was much impressed both by his confidence and his sensitivity. In return for my time and interest he sent me 'David's Harp'.

Presently I left the library service and became an Undergraduate at the London University, and for about three years, lost sight of Rosenberg. After I obtained my Degree, in about 1909, I met Rosenberg and discovered he was a student at the Bolt Court Art School, and for a number of weeks he, and artist called Daniels who disappeared in the War, and I, would spend many hours talking about books or pictures.

On the whole, I was rather disappointed in Rosenberg. He did not seem to me to realise the exceptional promise of his boyhood, but I always found him an exceedingly pleasant fellow, ready to give me the benefit of his knowledge and appreciation of pictures.

I last saw him in 1913, and by that time he had made friends with a Jewish artist called Amschewitz, a Jewish actor called Michael Sherbrooke, and interesting Jewish families such as the Solomons and the Delissa Josephs.* He gave me the impression that these Jewish families were much interested in his gifts, but that he was not particularly happy in mixing with them because he suspected a certain amount of patronage.

If these slender remarks are of any use to you, you may use them.

* IR's patrons (Chronology, p. 16).

If my delay in replying to your letter has prevented your use of them, I am sorry.

I am, Sir,

Yours faithfully

Morley Dainow.

Director, the Pelman Laboratory of Applied Psychology

6. Letter to Binyon from C. KoeChila, Professor's Assistant, on headed notepaper, dated 17 June 1921.

University of London

University College

Gower Street

London WC1

Dear Sir

Isaac Rosenberg entered this School in October 1911, and left in March 1914. He was enthusiastic in his work here, which certainly showed promise. He was skilful with the brush, and he gained a second Prize for Painting from the Head Model in the competitions, Session 1911–12.

I believe that he exhibited works in The New English Art Club, but I have not a record of this.

Pray let me know if I can help you further in the matter.

And I am,

Yours truly

C. KoeChila

Professor's Assistant.

June 1919. Memoir by Annie Rosenberg (later Mrs Wynick); manuscript in ink in Annie Rosenberg's hand, sent to Laurence Binyon.

Isaac Rosenberg was born in Bristol November 25th 1890 of humble Jewish parents. His father was a poor traveller who had no independent means but had to struggle hard to make both ends meet in the battle for existence.

When young Isaac was seven years of age, his parents came to London where they resided in the heart of the 'Ghetto'– St George's-in-the-East. Here his education began at an ordinary Board School, his parents being unable to cope with expenses entailed in a higher school. His early education thus, owing to unavoidable circumstances, neglected.

The Jews are a wandering sect of people & after a time Isaac was sent to another school – Baker St Stepney, whither his people had gone to reside. Isaac had always shown from his early childhood tendencies leaning towards the artistic as it was here at this school that his exceptional ability in Drawing and writing began to commend itself from a boy's standpoint. His headmaster took a special interest in him & allowed him to spend all his time at school in Drawing and writing! Even out of school hours this tendency for drawing would lead young Isaac to become a 'Pavement Artist' in the street, when he would portray several people, much to the amusement and consternation of crowds, which would assemble to watch him.

When 12 years of age, Isaac was full of zeal & energy in the pursuit of his Art which he always held dear to himself. On one occasion he made a mental vision of an old gentleman in the street – a passer-by, and so struck was he with his finely moulded head that he immediately reproduced it on paper on his arrival home. He was always fond of reading classical fiction & poetry, which he would often recite before, between & after meals.

At the age of 14 Isaac was very reluctantly compelled to leave school. His parents were poor & being a family of eight, the struggle for mere existence at times was a difficult problem to tax [? – word illegible].

Isaac was therefore now obliged to start the battle for existence. Upon leaving school he was apprenticed for five years to Messrs. Carl

Hentschel, Fleet St. London, in fine Art Etching. He was never happy at this work, but made himself happy during spare moments & mealtimes by writing poems, viz. 'Noon in the City': 'In the park' etc. etc. & in the evenings he attended the Art School Birkbeck College. Here he worked hard and gained many prizes & certificates. Realizing that every moment was precious if he was to approach his ambition, he studied morning till night with that zealousness that was so characteristic of him, either writing essays or poems, or sketching &c.

The term of apprenticeship with joy ended & he left.

His parents who were always so proud of him, extremely regretted their inability to offer him much assistance, & Isaac resolved to further his studies in Art, meeting with many great privations. He asked for assistance from the Jewish Free Education Society whose objects are to help further education where means were not available. This, he was refused.

He then made the acquaintance of two gentlemen, one, an artist, Amschewitz & the other Mr Samuels. Isaac was greatly indebted to these two gentlemen, who were really the first to place him on the right road. Through them, he made the acquaintance of Mrs Josephs (Solomon J. Solomon's RA sister) & subsequently Mrs Herbert Cohen & Mrs Lowy, who took great interest in him, & he was by their kind efforts, sent to the Slade School of Art – (I believe they paid all expenses & gave him pocket expenses).

Here too he distinguished himself, & Professor Brown thought very highly of him. At different periods, some of his paintings have been exhibited: one painting of his father exhibited at Whitechapel Art Gallery – London was highly commented on. He left this school in 1914: & then again began a very, very hard struggle for existence; but he would never admit defeat & was always painting & writing. On rare occasions he would sell a few pictures.

A few of his poems were published in 'The Poetry Review' Chicago & 'The Georgian Poetry' [sic]. He then made the acquaintance of a number of prominent gentlemen of of [sic] whom took a keen interest in him.

His health at this juncture gradually became indifferent (he had never enjoyed perfect health) & from neglect, he eventually developed lung trouble, which caused him to cough very vehemently at times. His health thus assuming an alarming character he was medically advised a sojourn in a warm climate & having a married sister in Africa, he left for Capetown [sic] in June 1914.

Unfortunately he did not attain great success here, where the public, the exception of a small minority, did not seem to be intellectual enough to grasp the beauty of his works. He made the acquaintance of Misses Molteno (Late Sir John Molteno's daughters) Rondesbosch, who took a great & keen interest in him & published a few articles written by Isaac in 'Art' & a few poems in the 'Women's S. African Journal' Cape Town. He returned to London disappointed with things in general, bringing with him a few paintings, including several fine 'heads' of the natives.

Upon his arrival he immediately took to writing & published a small volume of poems, 'Night & Day'.

At this period he suddenly became very restless, & although totally unfit to brave the rigours of Army Life, joined the forces in 1915 at the height of the war. However, Isaac managed to continue his writings, under most trying circumstances, & was compelled with the exception of an occasional sketch, to give up his passion for paintings. He thus devoted all his spare time to his writings & brought out two small books, 'Youth & other poems': 'Moses' a play.

Early in 1916 he was sent to France with the Kings Own Royal Lancasters where with his physical inaptitude, endured [sic] all the hardships of modern warfare.

While in the Trenches his ardent desire to pen his thoughts manifested itself & he produced some realistic poems, the best of which were 'Daughters of War', 'The Dead Man's Dump' [sic], 'In War'.

The last work of his, which was done in the trenches, was a water colour panel of himself; entitled by him 'The New Fashion boiler hat' – the trench hat [sic]. He was killed in action on April 1 1918.

He was always of a highly sensitive nature, very sincere & modest – but full of good humour, which often acted as a cloak to hide the grim realities and struggles he was called upon to face in life.

He was so reserved that even to his dearest relatives he would never discuss things that were eating his young heart out. He always had the greatest confidence in himself & was convinced that his ambition was not far off. To his mother he always had a cheery word in the direst of circumstances & would often say, 'Don't worry Ma, when I have something good – you will know it.'

Many things we discovered from outside sources, so I am unable to acquaint you with many other details of his life, which I feel sure would have been of great interest.

This history is not written sufficiently well to do my poor brother full justice, as I feel too choked to think that I write this in 'memory of my dear brother'.

Annie Rosenberg.

Appendix

The Poems: published final versions

The Troop Ship

Grotesque and queerly huddled
Contortionists to twist
The sleepy soul to a sleep,
We lie all sorts of ways
But cannot sleep.   5
The wet wind is so cold,
And the lurching men so careless,
That, should you drop to a doze,
Wind's fumble or men's feet
Is on your face.   10

Break of Day in the Trenches

The darkness crumbles away,
It is the same old Druid Time as ever.
Only a live thing leaps my hand,
A queer sardonic rat,
As I pull the parapet's poppy   5
To stick behind my ear.
Droll rat, they would shoot you if they knew
Your cosmopolitan sympathies.
Now you have touched this English hand,
You will do the same to a German   10
Soon, no doubt, if it be your pleasure
To cross the sleeping green between.
It seems, odd thing, you grin as you pass

Strong eyes, fine limbs, haughty athletes,
Less chanced than you for life,   15
Helpless whims of murder,
Sprawled in the bowels of the earth,
The torn fields of France.
What do you see in our eyes
At the shrieking iron and flame   20
Hurl'd through still heavens?
What quaver – what heart aghast?
Poppies whose roots are in man's veins
Drop, and are ever dropping,
But mine in my ear is safe –   25
Just a little white with the dust.

Pozières

Glory! glory! glory!
British women! in your wombs you plotted
This monstrous girth of glory, this marvellous glory.
Not for mere love-delights Time meant the profound hour
When an Englishman was planned.   5
Time shouted it to his extremest outpost.
The illuminated call through the voided years
Was heard, is heard at last,
And will be heard at the last
Reverberated through the Eternities,   10
Earth's immortality and Heaven's.

The Destruction of Jerusalem by the Babylonian Hordes

They left their Babylon bare
Of all its tall men.
Of all its proud horses;
They made for Lebanon.

And shadowy sowers went   5
Before their spears to sow
The fruit whose taste is ash
For Judah's soul to know.

They who bowed to the Bull god,
Whose wings roofed Babylon   10
In endless hosts darkened
The bright-heavened Lebanon.

They washed their grime in pools
Where laughing girls forgot
The wiles they used for Solomon.   15
Sweet laughter! remembered not.

Sweet laughter charred in the flame
That clutched the cloud and earth
While Solomon's towers crashed between
The gird of Babylon's mirth.   20

The Jew

Moses, from whose loins I sprung,
Lit by a lamp in his blood
Ten immutable rules, a moon
For mutable lampless men.

The blonde, the bronze, the ruddy,   5
With the same heaving blood,
Keep tide to the moon of Moses,
Then why do they sneer at me?

Daughters of War

Space beats the ruddy freedom of their limbs –
Their naked dances with man's spirit naked
By the root side of the tree of life.
(The underside of things
And shut from earth's profoundest eyes).   5

I saw in prophetic gleams
These mighty daughters in their dances
Beckon each soul aghast from its crimson corpse
To mix in their glittering dances.
I heard the mighty daughters' giant sighs   10
In sleepless passion for the sons of valour,
And envy of the days of flesh
Barring their love with mortal boughs across, –
The mortal boughs – the mortal tree of life,
The old bark burnt with iron wars   15
They blow to a live flame
To char the young green days
And reach the occult soul; – they have no softer lure –
No softer lure than the savage ways of death.
We were satisfied of our Lords the moon and the sun   20
To take our wage of sleep and bread and warmth –
These maidens came – these strong everliving Amazons,
And in an easy might their wrists
Of night's sway and noon's sway the sceptres brake,
Clouding the wild – the soft lustres of our eyes.   25

Clouding the wild lustres, the clinging tender lights;
Driving the darkness into the flame of day,
With the Amazonian wind of them
Over our corroding faces
That must be broken – broken for evermore   30
So that the soul can leap out
Into their huge embraces.
Tho' there are human faces
Best sculptures of Deity,
And sinews lusted after   35
By the Archangels tall,
Even these must leap to the love-heat of these maidens
From the flame of terrene days,
Leaving gray ashes to the wind – to the wind.

One (whose great lifted face,   40
Where wisdom's strength and beauty's strength
And the thewed strength of large beasts
Moved and merged, gloomed and lit)
Was speaking, surely, as the earth-men's earth fell away;
Whose new hearing drunk the sound   45
Where pictures lutes and mountains mixed
With the loosed spirit of a thought.
Essenced to language, thus –

'My sisters force their males
From the doomed earth, from the doomed glee   50
And hankering of hearts.
Frail hands gleam up through the human quagmire,
    and lips of ash
Seem to wail, as in sad faded paintings
Far sunken and strange.
My sisters have their males   55
Clean of the dust of the old days
That clings about those white hands,

And yearns in voices sad.
But these shall not see them,
Or think of them in any days or years,   60
They are my sister's lovers in other days and years.'

Dead Man's Dump

The plunging limbers over the shattered track
Racketed with their rusty freight,
Stuck out like many crowns of thorns,
And the rusty stakes like sceptres old
To stay the flood of brutish men   5
Upon our brothers dear.

The wheels lurched over sprawled dead
But pained them not, though their bones crunched,
Their shut mouths made no moan,
They lie there huddled, friend and foeman,   10
Man born of man, and born of woman,
And shells go crying over them
From night till night and now.

Earth has waited for them
All the time of their growth   15
Fretting for their decay:
Now she has them at last!
In the strength of their strength
Suspended – stopped and held.

What fierce imaginings their dark souls lit   20
Earth! Have they gone into you?
Somewhere they must have gone,
And flung on your hard back
Is their soul's sack,

Emptied of God-ancestralled essences.   25
Who hurled them out? Who hurled?

None saw their spirits' shadow shake the grass,
Or stood aside for the half used life to pass
Out of those doomed nostrils and the doomed mouth,
When the swift iron burning bee   30
Drained the wild honey of their youth.

What of us, who flung on the shrieking pyre,
Walk, our usual thoughts untouched,
Our lucky limbs as on ichor fed,
Immortal seeming ever?   35
Perhaps when the flames beat loud on us,
A fear may choke in our veins
And the startled blood may stop.

The air is loud with death,
The dark air spurts with fire   40
The explosions ceaseless are.
Timelessly now, some minutes past,
These dead strode time with vigorous life,
Till the shrapnel called 'an end!'
But not to all. In bleeding pangs   45
Some borne on stretchers dreamed of home,
Dear things, war-blotted from their hearts.

A man's brains splattered on
A stretcher-bearer's face;
His shook shoulders slipped their load,   50
But when they bent to look again
The drowning soul was sunk too deep
For human tenderness.

They left this dead with the older dead,
Stretched at the cross roads.   55

Burnt black by strange decay
Their sinister faces lie
The lid over each eye,
The grass and coloured clay
More motion have than they,   60
Joined to the great sunk silences.

Here is one not long dead;
His dark hearing caught our far wheels,
And the choked soul stretched weak hands,
To reach the living word the far wheels said,   65
The blood-dazed intelligence beating for light,
Crying through the suspense of the far-torturing wheels
Swift for the end to break,
Or the wheels to break,
Cried as the tide of the world broke over his sight.   70

Will they come? Will they ever come?
Even as the mixed hoofs of the mules,
The quivering-bellied mules,
And the rushing wheels all mixed
With his tortured upturned sight,   75
So we crashed round the bend,
We heard his weak scream,
We heard his very last sound,
And our wheels grazed his dead face.

Girl to Soldier on Leave

I love you – Titan lover,
My own storm-days' Titan.
Greater than the son of Zeus,
I know who I would choose.

Titan – my splendid rebel –   5
The old Prometheus
Wanes like a ghost before your power –
His pangs were joys to yours.

Pallid days arid and wan
Tied your soul fast.   10
Babel cities' smoky tops
Pressed upon your growth

Weary gyves. What were you,
But a word in the brain's ways,
Or the sleep of Circe's swine.   15
One gyve holds you yet. –

It held you hiddenly on the Somme
Tied from my heart at home.
O must it loosen now? – I wish
You were bound with the old old gyves.   20

Love! you love me – your eyes
Have looked through death at mine.
You have tempted a grave too much.
I let you – I repine.

In War

Fret the nonchalant noon
With your spleen
Or your gay brow,
For the motion of thy spirit
Ever moves with these.   5

When day shall be too quiet,
Deaf to you
And your dumb smile,
Untuned air shall lap the stillness
In the old space for your voice –   10

The voice that once could mirror
Remote depths
Of moving being,
Stirred by responsive voices near,
Suddenly stilled for ever.   15

No ghost darkens the places
Dark to One;
But my eyes dream,
And my heart is heavy to think
How it was heavy once.   20

In the old days when death
Stalked the world
For the flower of men,
And the rose of beauty faded
And pined in the great gloom,   25

One day we dug a grave:
We were vexed
With the sun's heat.
We scanned the hooded dead:
At noon we sat & talked   30

How death had kissed their eyes
Three dread noons since,
How human art won
The dark soul to flicker
Till it was lost again: 35

And we whom chance kept whole –
But haggard,
Spent – were charged
To make a place for them who knew
No pain in any place.   40

The good priest came to pray:
Our ears half heard,
And half we thought
Of alien things, irrelevant;
And the heat and thirst were great.   45

The good priest read: 'I heard . . .'
Dimly my brain
Held words and lost . . .
Suddenly my blood ran cold . . .
God! God! It could not be.   50

He read my brother's name;
I sank –
I clutched the priest.
They did not tell me it was he
Was killed three days ago.   55

What are the great sceptred dooms
To us, caught
In the wild wave?
We break ourselves on them,
My brother, our hearts and years.   60

The Tower of Skulls

These layers of piled-up skulls,
These layers of gleaming horror – stark horror!
Ah me! Through my thin hands they touch my eyes.

Everywhere, everywhere is a pregnant birth,
And here in death's land is a pregnant birth.   5
Your own crying is less mortal
Than the amazing soul in your body.

Your own crying yon parrot takes up
And from your empty skulls cries it afterwards.

Thou whose dark activities unenchanted   10
Days from gyrating days, suspending them
To thrust them far from sight, from the gyrating days
Which have gone widening on & left us here,
Cast derelicts lost for ever.

When aged flesh looks down on tender brood;   15
For he knows between his thin ribs' walls
The giant universe, the interminable
Panorama – synods, myths and creeds,
He knows his dust is fire and seed.

The Dying Soldier

'Here are houses' he moaned,
'I could reach but my brain swims'.
Then they thundered and flashed
And shook the earth to its rims.

'They are gunpits' he gasped,   5
'Our men are at the guns.
Water . . Water . . O water
For one of England's dying sons'.

'We cannot give you water
Were all England in your breath'.   10
'Water! . . Water! . . O! Water!'
He moaned and swooned to death.

The Burning of the Temple

Fierce wrath of Solomon
Where sleepest thou? O see
The fabric which thou won
Earth and ocean to give thee –
O look at the red skies.   5

Or hath the sun plunged down?
What is this molten gold –
These thundering fires blown
Through heaven – where the smoke rolled.
Again the great king dies.   10

His dreams go out in smoke,
His days he let not pass
And sculptured here are broke
Are charred as the burnt grass
Gone as his mouth's last sighs.   15

Returning, We Hear The Larks

Sombre the night is.
And though we have our lives, we know
What sinister threat lurks there.

Dragging these anguished limbs, we only know
This poison-blasted track opens on our camp –   5
On a little safe sleep.

But hark! joy – joy – strange joy.
Lo! heights of night ringing with unseen larks.
Music showering our upturned list'ning faces.

Death could drop from the dark   10
As easily as song –
But song only dropped,
Like a blind man's dreams on the sand
By dangerous tides,
Like a girl's dark hair for she dreams no ruin lies there,   15
Or her kisses where a serpent hides.